ALL IN THE FAMILY

75 YEARS OF WINGFIELD PREACHING

REV. DR. RICHARD WINGFIELD

urbanpress

All in the Family: 75 Years of Wingfield Preaching
by Rev. Dr. Richard Wingfield
Copyright ©2017 Rev. Dr. Richard Wingfield

Church images courtesy of Google

ISBN 978-1-63360-071-3
For Worldwide Distribution
Printed in the U.S.A.

Urban Press
P.O. Box 8881
Pittsburgh, PA 15221-0881
412.646.2780

To Vanessa, my friend, my queen, my wife

PREFACE

"How, then, can they call on the one they have not believed in?
And how can they believe in the one of whom they have not heard?
And how can they hear without someone preaching to them?
And how can they preach unless they are sent? As it is written,
How beautiful are they feet of those who bring good news?'"
- Romans 10:14-15 (NIV).

I remember it vividly, like it happened yesterday. I was a young preacher's kid sitting in church. My father was the pastor and my mother was the church organist. I knew my father worked on his sermon all week long, and was up late Saturday night putting the final touches on Sunday's sermonic presentation. Then came Sunday morning. He would mount the sacred space, robed and ready to lead in worship. The culmination of the worship was the preached word and the invitation to discipleship. My father would powerfully and passionately preach, extending the privilege of membership in the church. Oftentimes, no one would respond to the call. On those Sundays, just before pronouncing the benediction, he would cite some words that resonate in my spirit to this day: "We have done as has been commanded. If Israel isn't saved, Jacob shall not lose his reward."

I'm not clear where this saying came from. Yet, these words suggested that the faithful proclamation of the word of God called for a response from the hearer. If the proclaimer is faithful and the hearer does not respond to salvation, the blood is not on the proclaimer's hands, but on the hands of the hearer.

For more than seventy-five years, the Wingfield name has been synonymous with preaching in the southwestern area of Pennsylvania. We responded to the call of God to preach the gospel, and some great sermons have fallen from the lips of the Wingfields, in particular from my forebears. Because of the tremendous heritage of preaching, it was my desire to honor this heritage in print.

All of the Wingfields were manuscript preachers, and each one had his own unique style of manuscript development. These manuscripts, however, were prepared not to be read, but to be both heard and experienced by the hearer. A number of sermons have been preserved through the years; some were handwritten and some were typed, their paper beginning to deteriorate. These sermons were handed down to each new generation of Wingfield preachers. From these manuscripts, the best and most notable are entered into this volume. These sermons are printed as closely to the original typed or written version as possible with only minor editing.

This volume must be read with the African-American context in mind. The black dialogue or the "call/response" is a given in African-American preaching. There is a dynamic in this dialogue that takes the black preacher to another level and allows for that which is not written on paper to be expressed in the sermonic presentation—what the preacher of antiquity referred to as "heavenly airmail delivered by the Spirit of God."

My family believed the Scriptures were the authority on which we stood to proclaim the word of God. This is evidenced through the frequent use of Bible passages throughout each manuscript. The sermons entered into this volume were chosen based on specific criteria: 1) their noteworthiness or the notations attached to these sermons; 2) the significance of the events of that time; and 3) their ability to inspire and motivate the listener and now the reader.

There are many faithful proclaimers of the gospel who are not known for their national prominence or for the masses that come through the doors of their respective churches. Instead, they are renowned for their faithfulness to the call of God. Such is the case with the Wingfield preachers. None of us attained national prominence and our congregations were never defined as megachurches. In spite of that, we were faithful to the proclamation of the word of God where we ministered. Whenever people would leave the hallowed walls of the sanctuary on Sunday after a Wingfield had preached, they knew they had heard a word from the Lord.

The words of the familiar hymn of Charles Wesley epitomized the response of our call and appear to comprise our family motto. I remember this hymn being "lined," that is, sung in the old-fashioned, meter style common to the African-American experience:

A charge to keep I have, God to glorify,
A never-dying soul to save, and fit it for the sky.
To serve the present age, my calling to fulfill:
Oh may it all my powers engage to do my Master's will!
Arm me with jealous care, as in Thy sight to live;
And Oh Thy servant, Lord, prepare a strict account to give!
Help me to watch and pray, and on Thyself rely,
Assured, if I my trust betray, I shall forever die.
—*A Charge I Have to Keep* by Charles Wesley.

It is my prayer that through this printed material, the heritage of the Wingfield family will be preserved, that these sermons may plant a seed and stimulate the thought of other laborers in the gospel in their sermon preparation, and that lives may be touched and ever changed through these words from the Eternal One of glory.

Special Acknowledgment

In researching this project, it was found that another Wingfield served as a pastor in the Pittsburgh area, The Reverend Albert Wingfield, who was the brother of W. W. Wingfield, Sr. and my great uncle, served as the pastor of the First Baptist Church of Finleyville, Pennsylvania during the 1920s.

Mrs. Mae Ellen Green, a life-long member of this congregation, was baptized by Reverend Albert Wingfield, and shared some history that much of the family was not aware of. While delivering the morning sermon, he leaned over the pulpit and said, "Brother and sisters, I don't feel very well." Having made this statement, he collapsed in the pulpit. The deacons carried him back to his home in Pittsburgh by trolley car where he expired later that evening.[1] There were no sermons preserved from that era, however, we pause to acknowledge my great-uncle's commission as another great proclaimer of the gospel in the Wingfield tradition.

---

[1] At the time of this conversation, Mrs. Green was in her 90s and had been the pianist of this church for 81 years.

INTRODUCTION

Black preaching in general and the sermons you are about to read in particular before you actually read them. Black preaching is known as some of the most powerful preaching on the American scene. The preaching of the Black cleric has been known to inspire, challenge, motivate, and transform the lives of the hearers. Though there are those who make a mockery of it, their mockery only hides their secret love and appreciation for it.

The Black pulpit is known as the freest pulpit in America. It is free because of its ability to speak truth to power and to address the social issues of the day from a biblical viewpoint. The Black preacher did not stand in his own authority, but when he spoke, he spoke "thus saith the Lord." Therefore, the Black preacher was the freest man of all, for from his pulpit he could speak out against the evils corrupting Christianity in America. It was perhaps the only place from which truly prophetic Christianity could be propagated.[2]

The strength of Black preaching is its hermeneutic flexibility and its homiletic ingenuity. Black preaching interprets the text from a Black perspective and allows for a certain amount of creative liberty with the text. It is not eisegesis [reading into the text], but it allows the text to speak in specific ways to certain situations. In doing so, the preacher is using his or her "sanctified imagination" to bring a prophetic word for the moment.

Sermon Analysis

The meticulous development of each sermon is evident. Each one valued reading and labored over the content of the sermon. Content and careful preparation are vitally important to the preaching event. It is my belief, and indeed I was taught, that the conclusion did not mean much if there was no content to justify the conclusion.

The use of language was very important. Each one agonized over the words they would use in the pulpit. Henry Mitchell relates the importance of language to the Black listener: "If we want God to be real to black people linguistics must also be used to present a picture of God to whom they can relate."[3] I never heard my grandfather preach, but I marvel as I read his poetic use of language and his use of imagery in his sermons. The evidence is clear that there was a struggle over language in the preaching of my father and uncle. This was further confirmed by a family friend who mentioned how they would call each other three or four times a week and preach their sermons over the phone to each other. It should be noted that the sermons of the elder Wingfields were preached before inclusive language ever became an issue in the African-American church, but they nonetheless were aware of the power of language.

---

[2]Nelson Hart, *The Black Church in America.* (New York: Basic Books, 1971), p. 287.

[3]Emanuel McCall, *Black Church Lifestyles: Rediscovering the Black Christian Experience.* (Nashville: Broadman Press, 1986), p.122.

Delivery and Style

Each one's preaching style was unique to his own personality. A key factor in the development of style and the strengthening of one's own preaching ability is exposure to other preachers. As one is exposed to the preaching of others, a person's own style is developed, and each on the preachers deliberately sought to expose himself to some of the best preaching nationwide. All were methodical in their sermonic delivery.

The Climax and Celebration

Each individual climax is distinct. It is common knowledge that God uses the personality of each as they deliver His word. One should never seek to be a clone of another. One of the indictments, as well as weaknesses, of Black preaching is the desire among many to imitate another well-known preacher in delivery and, in particular, the climax of the sermon. Many good sermons have been ruined by telegraphed, mimicked climaxes void of the Spirit's anointing and, in some cases, having nothing to do with the content of the sermon.

The "whoop," the tonal closing of the Black sermon, in the words of one preacher, was letting Grandma know that everything will be alright in the morning. Certainly, this is a part of the cultural experience of African Americans. Yet, it is my contention that Grandma also needs to know how to make it through the night, and this comes with solid preaching.

I am told that my grandfather was a "whooper" and had a deep, resonant voice to go along with it. Ironically, neither son took up the traditional "whoop" though they had their own way of climaxing a sermon. A. L. Wingfield would often close his message by saying, "I'm through, I'm not finished, but I'm through." My father would often quote Ecclesiastes 12:13 as he began his conclusion. Occasionally I engage in the "whoop." According to one observer, when I do, I tend to sneak up on the hearer.

The climax, regardless of how it is done, is proof to the hearer that there is hope. Black preaching produces a theology of the suffering servant and a gospel of future hope. Through the climax, the hearer's faith is affirmed and "the worshippers would share vicariously in the freedom of the preacher, to the extent that he does just what he feels like doing. They enjoy this."[4]

The Evolution of Preaching

"'All souls are mine,' says the Lord" (Ezekiel 18:4). The gospel has a universal flavor to it and reaches beyond the cultural boundaries to every individual. The message of the gospel transcends racial, ethnic, cultural, political, and social biases. This "whosoever will" gospel teaches the availability of salvation for all who would call on the name of the Lord.

The social and political climate, however, has some bearing on the preaching moment. The content of these sermons has evolved over the years as the manuscripts in this volume reveals. Preaching has evolved from a universal preachment of the gospel to preaching for the purposes of raising Black consciousness. It has evolved from just soul salvation to a more holistic approach, a preaching that reaches the whole person. God is revealed as the God of the oppressed. Even though the universality of the gospel is present, there is the sense in which the gospel is preached for those

---

[4]*Ibid.*, p. 120.

whose backs are against the wall—those whose main purpose is to survive. Luke 4:18-19 becomes the cry of the preacher: "The Spirit of the Lord is on me, because he has anointed me to proclaim good news to the poor. He has sent me to proclaim freedom for the prisoners and recovery of sight for the blind, to set the oppressed free, to proclaim the year of the Lord's favor."

The preaching has also evolved due to the affluence of African Americans. If prophetic preaching is a call to bring people back to God, the emphasis is now on getting people to remember where we have come from and to challenge the Black soul to look back and wonder how we made it over. The social and political climate affected our preaching, especially that of my father. The sermons of my father seemed to be more on the side of Black liberation theology, though he did not embrace all of its tenets. I lean toward this theological approach to Scripture.

The social context affected the preaching more than the national ecclesiastical context. In the sermons presented, the ecclesiastical concerns were not addressed per se, though there was concern regarding the state of the church as a whole. The issues that were transpiring on the national level did not seem to faze their preaching.

Social concerns, injustices, and race prejudice were prevalent themes. I saw this more in my father's manuscripts than in my grandfather and uncle. Though the sermons in my possession do not reveal this, I am told that both were relevant in their preaching, addressing the issues of the day. As stated earlier, there are things that are not written in a manuscript that come out in the sermon.

The overarching concern expressed in the preaching of all was the issue of survival. This is a common thread throughout all of the sermons. How can I survive in the midst of racial tensions and prejudice? How can I survive when I am laid off of my job, the company is downsizing, the bills are due, and the unemployment runs out? My grandfather's preaching emphasized keeping the faith until the consummation of things. It looked forward to that day when all things are made new and God shall wipe all tears from their eyes. Preaching the hope of "someday" seemed to be my family's generation's theology of survival. Later generations, however, did not focus on this eschatological approach. We seemed to place emphasis on believing God will provide what I need to make it now.

The Recovery of a Passion for Preaching

I am convinced that there must be a recovery of the passion for preaching. In a day when there are preachers who have gone AWOL and where there are those who become prophets for profit, it is imperative that a passion for preaching be recovered. The preacher of this day must begin to take preaching seriously.

Preaching is the divinely-ordained means by which one can hear the message of the gospel. The Apostle Paul tells us, "It pleased God by the foolishness of preaching to save them that believe" (1 Corinthians 1:21).

This does not suggest that preaching is foolish, and neither does it condone foolish preaching. Thus, preaching ought not to be taken lightly. The call to preach is a serious call and the activity of preaching is essential to salvation. Thus, it must be approached with a reverent awe for the One who has called us.

There are so many difficulties that the preacher endures that can easily rob him or her of spiritual vitality and passion as representative sons and daughters of God. When the people are before us on Sunday, they have come with the eternal question on their hearts and minds, "Is there a word from the Lord?" When we consider the souls of those who sit before us each week, we must echo the words of Paul, "Necessity is laid upon me; woe is me if I preach not the gospel of Christ" (1 Corinthians 9:16).

If passion is to be regained, there must be a sitting before the Lord in prayerful meditation. People come to hear a fresh word from the Lord. They are not looking for leftovers. Passionate preaching is relevant preaching that speaks to the times in which we live. It is preaching that reaches all ages. Passionate preaching is preaching that challenges people to move from where they are to where God wants them to be.

I guess you can say I am a chip off of the old block. Like my forebearers, I love good preaching, will travel miles to hear good preaching, and, like my ancestors, am very selective about who I allow to preach across the pulpit where God has placed me.

As mentioned earlier, I never heard my grandfather preach. He expired before I was old enough to understand what it was all about. My father never heard me preach. He died just four days before I was to preach my initial sermon. I had just preached my uncle's twenty-sixth pastoral anniversary at the Vermont Baptist Church when, one week later, he was called from labor to reward. Yet, I never realized the magnitude of their sermons until I took the time to read them. I have a greater appreciation for the heritage they left me, their passion for preaching, and their respective ministries.

SECTION ONE
REV. W. W. WINGFIELD, SR.

Reverend W. W. Wingfield, Sr., my grandfather, was a thirty-three-year veteran of the pulpit. Born December 6, 1898 in Fairfax County, Virginia, his preaching career began in 1929 as the assistant pastor of the Mt. Zion Baptist Church of Bluefield, West Virginia. He also served as pastor of the Golden Baptist Church of Princeton, Virginia for five years.

In 1937, he moved to Pittsburgh, Pennsylvania and became the pulpit assistant of the Macedonia Baptist Church of Pittsburgh. In 1939, he was called to pastor the First Baptist Church of Finleyville, Pennsylvania where he served for seven years.

In 1949, he was called to the Trinity Baptist Church in the Lawrenceville section of Pittsburgh. Under his administration, he led the congregation in building a new church edifice. The many activities he participated in included serving as president of the Baptist Minister's Conference of Pittsburgh and Vicinity. My grandfather was also one of the founding members of the Allegheny Union Baptist Association. Reverend Wingfield died suddenly on April 17, 1964 as the Trinity Baptist Church was preparing to honor him for fifteen years of service.

My grandfather preached during the years when segregation was at its apex. "Separate but equal" was the rule of the day, and the Civil Rights Movement was just taking shape. The Brown versus the Topeka Board of Education Supreme Court decision was years from happening as was the Montgomery bus boycott. Along with the social crises of the day, America was in the midst of World War II and, subsequently, the Korean conflict. Yet W. W. Wingfield, Sr. issued a strong clarion call to the people of his time. A preacher par-excellence and a pastor of the first magnitude, he preached the word of the Lord with power and conviction. He was a flat-footed preacher with melodic resonance and a strong voice that rang out across the city of Pittsburgh as will be evidenced by the following sermons.

LISTENING FOR A MESSAGE FROM GOD

**"I will stand upon my watch, and set upon the tower,
and I will listen to hear what God will say to me" (Habakkuk 2:1).**

In this imminent, threatening age of rockets and missiles that are being hurled into the air, giving evidence of impending danger to the health and safety of the human race, many ears are tuned to the political listening post to see if there is any word of security from the great and outstanding rulers of the world. In this momentous space age, when the nations are trying to be the first to land and live on the moon, millions of ears are listening to hear what the astronauts have to tell us about outer space; its structure, size, distance, and relative positions and courses through space.

To our rushing, scrambling, intensive, and noisy world, Habakkuk preaches a much-needed sermon. Instead of taxing our physical and mental powers to learn what world leaders and dictators are saying, we need, in a time like the one in which we live, to tune in on heaven and hear what "thus saith the Lord." For God is still on the throne. He is still in control of the universe and all power is still in His hands.

Nothing definite is known of this noble man, Habakkuk; who he was or what tribe he was from; where or how he lived is not recorded. However, we are brought to realize from the writings of this prophet that his richly-endowed life was not an easy one. We are certain that doubt and fear had harassed his very soul, bathing it in burning tears while discouragement swept over it like a wasting flood. But in spite of all of this, this brave soul did not despair but rose triumphant, singing the words of the text, "I will stand upon my watch, and set me upon the tower, and will listen to hear what God will say to me."

This listening denotes that the prophet was listening for a sound from above, from around and from within himself that he may not lose instructions or directions that the Spirit would dictate to him. He was anxious to gain intelligence, so he listened attentively for a word from God and carefully observed the steps of His providence.

It is also intimated that, even in an ordinary way, God not only speaks to us by his Word, but speaks in us by our own conscience, whispering to us, "*This* is the way, walk in it." The prophet, standing upon his tower or high place, shows his prudence by making use of the helps and means he had within his reach: to know the mind of God and to be instructed concerning it.

Those who expect to hear from God must withdraw from the world and get above it. They must raise their attention, fix their thoughts, study the Scriptures, consult experience and the experienced, and be instant in prayer, thus setting themselves upon the tower.

The prophet, standing upon his tower, imitates [God's] patience, His constancy, and resolution. He will wait the time and weather the point. He will know what God will say to him, not only for his satisfaction, but to enable him as a prophet to give satisfaction and consolation to others.

Herein is the prophet an example to us. When we are tossed and perplexed with doubt, when we are tempted to think that all is fate or fortune and there is not a wise God who governs the world, or that the church is abandoned and God's covenant with His people canceled and laid aside, it is here that we should ascend our tower and we will hear God say,

> "The vision is yet for an appointed time, but, at the end it shall speak and not lie: though it tarry, wait for it because it will surely come. And, until it comes, 'The just shall live by faith'" (Habakkuk 2:3-4).

Point One

The secret of life's success is to realize the being of God.

"I will stand at my watch, and station myself on the ramparts" (Habbakuk 2:1a).

The first words in the Bible are these: "In the beginning, God . . ." Here the great and important fact of creation is declared along with the sublimest of all truth—the existence of God. We must admit the being or the existence of God is a mystery that neither men nor angels can comprehend. For we cannot, by searching, find out God.

The measure thereof is longer than the earth and broader than the sea. But while we are lost in wonder, there is a Being who existed from eternity, and all the causes of His existence are in Himself. We should give glad welcome to the truth that there is a God and say with Paul, "For of him and through him, and by him, are all things to whom be glory forever" (Romans 11:36).

The being of God, though a mystery, furnishes the key that unlocks thousands of other mysteries. Because there is a God in heaven, man can know something about the universe, how it came into existence, and how it continues to exist. "In the beginning, God created the heavens and the earth."

And the world continues to exist on the same word that spoke it into existence. If the world, with its vastness, its beauty and splendor, can depend on God, why cannot we, weak and finite creatures, stretch out on His word?

We need, more than anything else, to fill our minds and hearts with God. To realize that He is in our being, and that in Him we live, move and have our being, and that whatever problem or difficulty may be ours to bear, an Almighty God is in control.

It would be to our advantage to realize that God is interwoven in the texture of all that He has made. His goodness blooms every flower, His glory beams every star, the sun speaks of His splendor every day, and the moon in her radiance portrays Him every night.

Yes, nature presents Jehovah. He can be seen in the smallest pebble on the beach, as well as in the orb that shines in the vaulted sky. He can be seen in the tiniest insect as well as in the master beast of the forest. His majesty commands the cherubim. His arm is around the world and His temple is filled with His glory. It is no wonder David exclaimed in Psalm 19:1-4:

> "The heavens declares the glory of God; and the firmament showeth his handiwork. Day unto day uttereth speech and night unto night showeth knowledge. There is no speech nor language where their voice is not heard; their line is gone out through all the earth and the words to the ends of the world."

Like Moses, if we can realize the presence of God amidst the ordinary things of life, bush may suddenly catch fire and any desert may bloom prolifically with His beauty. May we say with Charles H. Scott,

> "Open my eyes that I may see,
> Glimpses of truth Thou hast for me;
> Place in my hand the wonderful key
> That shall unclasp and set me free.
> Open my ears that I may hear,
> Voices of truth Thou sendest clear;
> And while the wave-note fall on my ear,
> Everything false will disappear.
> Silently, now, I wait for Thee,
> Ready, my God, Thy will to see;
> Open my heart, illumine me,
> Spirit Divine."

Point Two

We ought to listen for a message from God.

"I will hear what the Lord will say to me" (Habbakuk 2:1b).

This unseen One is no dumb god like the gods of the heathens. Rather, He is One who has something to say to all who have ears to hear. To every prophet, preacher, pastor, and teacher, as well as the whole human race, God has a message for you.

To the prophet, God is saying, "Prophesy to these dry bones," the spiritually dry and indifferent in the household of faith, to "hear the word of the Lord." To the preacher he says,

> "Preach the word, be instant in season, out of season; reprove, rebuke, exhort with all long-suffering and doctrine. For the time will come when they will not endure sound doctrine. But watch, thou, in all things, endure afflictions, do the work of an evangelist, make full proof of thy ministry" (2 Timothy 4:2-5).

To the teacher, God's message rings clear: "Go ye, therefore, and teach all nations, teaching them to observe all things, whatsoever I have commanded you; and, lo, I am with you always, even unto the end of the world" (Matthew 28:19).

To the pastors, God speaks, "Take heed, therefore, unto yourselves, and to all the flock over which the Holy Ghost has made you overseers, to feed the church of God which he purchased with his own blood" (Acts 20:28).

God has something to say, not only to the prophets, preachers, pastors, and teachers, but also to the human family. He desires to talk with us about His love for the human race: "For God so loved the world that He gave his only begotten son, that whosoever believeth in him should not perish but have everlasting life" (John 3:16).

I shall never be able to comprehend the vastness of these words, "God so loved the world." Like the smallest fish that swims in the boundless ocean, however, we shall not concern ourselves with the insurmountable depth, but plunge with our puny capacity into the immensity of God's love that we cannot comprehend. This is a love that does all things: that brings to pass even the evil we suffer, so shaping them that they are but instruments of preparing the good which has not yet arrived.

Pause, fellow travelers, before this wonderful Being who was found in a manger, on a cross, in a grave. Follow His footsteps, dwell in His Word, listen to His prayer, gaze on His tears and on the blood that flowed freely from His side, and you will recall that God loves when we do not love Him or ourselves.

God desires to converse with us concerning His omnipresence. There are regions, I am told, beyond the most nebulous outskirts of matter, but there are none beyond the being of God. Said the psalmist; "If I take the wings of the morning and fly to the utmost parts of the earth, there shall his right hand uphold me" (Psalm 139:9).

God is everywhere present by His power. He rolls the orb of heaven with His hand; He fixes the earth with His foot, He guides all creatures with His eye; and refreshes them with His influence. He makes the powers of hell to shake with His terror and binds the devil with His word.

The saints are assured by God's omnipresence that, whatever situation they may find themselves in, wherever they may be, whatever the consequence: "I am with you always, even to the end of the world" (Matthew 28:20). Because we are assured of His presence, we can sing as David did, "The Lord is my shepherd, I shall not want" (Psalm 23:1).

God would talk to us concerning His providence. The doctrine of God's providence should give full consolation to believers. For by it, they are assured that the universe is not under the dominion of unreasoning fate or blind chance. Fate and chance are impersonal. There is neither life nor intelligence in them. Let us be thankful that we have a personal God on the throne governing the universe, infinite in goodness, wisdom and power. And His eye is everywhere, beholding the good and the bad.

God would say to us that there will be a solution of the mysteries of His providence. The saying of Paul is profoundly true when he says, "For we know in part" (1 Corinthians 13:12b). For the present state of humanity is unfinished, imperfect, and needs to be supplemented by the knowledge of God's providential care.

Many of the works of providence are involved in obscurity and darkness. For it is written, "He holdeth back the face of his throne, and spreadest his cloud upon it, his way is in the sea, and his path in the great waters; what I do thou knowest not now, but thou shall know hereafter." We will understand it better by and by.

The trials of the saints, which now often crush their spirits and break their hearts, will, in due time, call forth rapturous hallelujahs. Then it will be seen that, "Our light afflictions, which are but for a moment, worketh for us a far more exceeding weight of glory" (2 Corinthians 4:17).

"Judge not the Lord by feeble sense,
But, trust him for his grace;
Behind a frowning providence
He hides a smiling face.
His purposes will ripen fast,
Unfolding every hour;

The bud may have a bitter taste,
But sweet will be the flower.
Blind unbelief is sure to error
And scone his work in vain;
God is his own interpreter,
And he will make it plain."

Point Three

How shall we dispose ourselves in order to receive a message from God?

"We must stand upon our watch, and set upon our tower" (Habbakuk 2:1).

There is no breathing room down below. For down here there is such a scramble for the world's reward, clamoring for the world's praise, catering for the world's applause, and playing to the grandstand until it is difficult to hear what the Lord would say to us.

But, like Habakkuk, if we would receive a message from God, we must get up above the crowd, above the crush and clamor of the world. We must raise our attention and fix our thoughts on things above. We must patiently "set" upon our tower, waiting until God gets ready to speak through us and to work in us. We must be constant in our resolves, willing to weather whatever storms may come that we might know for ourselves that God can and will make a way, and to be able to comfort those who mourn in Zion.

CONCLUSION

When you are weak and fearful, and feel as though you cannot go any further,
get up in your tower and you will hear God saying to you through his word,
"God is our refuge and strength, a very present help in trouble.
Therefore, we will not fear. . ."

When your health is impaired and people constantly remind you to take it easy, get up in your tower and Jehovah will speak to you and tell you that "they that wait upon the Lord shall renew their strength" (Isaiah 40:31).

When the water gets deep and there is no bridge spanning the chasm, get up in your tower and God will say to you as He did to Israel, "When through the deep water I cause thee to go, I will be with thee, and through the rivers they shall not overflow thee" (Isaiah 43:2).

When you are in the wilderness of doubt, blinded by dismays, fear, feebleness, lame because of the wear and tear of your soul, when enemies attack and you are not able to answer, get up in your tower and God will encourage your soul saying, "The wilderness and the solitary place shall be glad for them; and the desert shall rejoice and blossom as the rose. The eyes of the blind shall be opened, and the lame man shall leap as a hart, and the tongue of the dumb shall sing" (Isaiah 35:1).

When you feel all alone in the world, appearing that everyone has forsaken you, get up in your tower and Jesus will say to you, "Lo, I am with you always, even unto the end of the earth" (Matthew 28:20).

When you begin to think in terms of having to lay down this life, and we all must do that, get up in your tower and God's word will comfort you in this language: "If the earthly house of this tabernacle be dissolved, we have a building of God, a house not made with hands, eternal in the heavens" (2 Corinthians 5:1).

When burdens continue to press you down, when trials of this life seem ceaseless, when troubles of this life will not let up and you find yourself at the crossroads of doubt and despair, wondering how long, get up in your tower and you will hear God saying to you,

"Afterwhile it will all be over,
Afterwhile, the sun will shine;
Afterwhile, the clouds will pass over,
We will shout troubles over afterwhile."

Let us pray.

LADDERS THAT REACH TO HEAVEN

"And Jacob went out from Beersheba and went toward Haran. And he lighted upon a certain place and he tarried there all night because the sun was set; and he took of the stones of that place, and put them for his pillows, and lay down in that place to sleep. And he dreamed, and behold a ladder set up on the earth and the top of it reached heaven" (Genesis 28:10-13).

There never was a time or an age in the history of the world that men have striven to reach a desirable height or place in life than they do now. There never was a time or age that it was more necessary, when it was more essential, that men should strive for higher heights than now. But in order to reach desirable heights in life, men must pursue the right course. None should deceive themselves, thinking they can mount to higher heights by climbing on anything or anyone that comes their way.

This was true of the man in today's text, Jacob, who thought he could go up on anything. So he cheated his brother out of his birthright, and deceived his aged father and stole his brother's blessing. But Jacob found out, as many of us have and all of us will, that *you cannot do wrong and get by*.

Not only will Satan's ladder not take us anywhere, but it will keep us from getting anywhere. Jacob climbed these ladders that offered him ease and comfort at no cost. But they caused him to leave home and go out into a strange land among strange people, to climb the lonely mountain at night alone, to use stones for a pillow and the canopy of heaven for his cover.

But had he not climbed these false ladders, he could have remained at home and enjoyed the comforts that it offered. This story of Jacob is another reminder that "the way of the transgressor is hard" (Proverbs 13:15). Jacob, like all the rest of the human family, must "reap his harvest."

Point One

Ladders upon which no advancement can be made.

All things of the earth are earthly and because they are so, they can carry no higher than the earth. All ungodly acts are of the world and they, whatever they may offer, however beautiful the picture they may paint to us, have nothing for us to attain. Let us mention a few of these ladders that Satan is trying to make people believe that by climbing them they will get somewhere in life.

Worldly fame. Here is one thing that Satan has and still is using to deceive: "Make for yourself a name in this world." There is no criticism for someone admonishing men to be somebody. But Satan does not give to mankind the receipts for true fame. Therefore, his fame becomes only worldly and, at its best, can last for a while.

The highest greatness surviving time and stone is that which proceeds from the soul of men. Monarchs and cabinets, generals and admirals, with the pomp of court and circumstances of war, in the lapse of time, all disappear from sight. But the pioneers of truth, though poor and lowly, can never be forgotten. When such men as General Eisenhower shall have been forgotten, men will still be saying, "Abraham believed God and it was counted to him as righteousness" (Romans 4:3).

The ladder of pride. Pride is the master sin of the devil. There is no more passion that steals into the heart more imperceptibly and covers itself under more disguise than pride. Pride looks back nicely on what it has done, calculates its past deeds, and commits itself to rest and ease. But my friends, it's not what you have done that will merit the approbation of God, but what you are doing when He calls you to report. Pride is in direct opposition to humility. Having gained one height, she looks down on that which is beneath.

The ladder of selfishness. Selfishness is an act of being devoted to one's own interest while careless about the concern of others. How many people are there who are desirous of doing good and serving God but they want to serve in a way to suit themselves? They want to serve and possess Him but they are not willing to be possessed by Him. My friends, let us beware of no man more than ourselves, for we carry our worst enemy within.

Point Two

Ladders upon which advancements can be made and upon which we may reach heaven.

This ladder that Jacob saw in his vision was a type of Christ on which men can advance upwards in spite of hindrances and pull-backs from the devil. Jesus is credited with bringing many sons and daughters to glory. The blind, the halt, the lame, the outcast, lepers, adulterers, backsliders—all may make progress in heaven's way by getting on Jesus.

Repentance. This is the first rung on the Christian ladder and it is a very important one. For unless our feet stand firmly on the rung of repentance, one will not be able to make the others.

The damaging hypocrisy of this age is that man may slight this first step in Christianity and spread their zeal and energy in matters of ceremony and a form of godliness without possessing the power. John saw the importance of this first step when many of the Pharisees came to his baptismal services and he said to them, "Oh! Ye generation of vipers who hath warned you to flee from the wrath to come? Bring forth fruit meet for repentance" (Matthew 3:8).

Faith. This is the second rung of the ladder and it is the key that unlocks the cabinet of God's treasures. It is the King's messenger from the celestial world to bring all the supplies we need to climb this ladder to the fullness that is in Christ Jesus. This is seen in the angels moving up and down the ladder. It will give you friends when in trouble, bread when you are hungry, water when you are thirsty, strength when you are weak, calmness in your fear, a bridge when the waters are deep, peace in the storm and quietness when waves are dashing high.

Love. The third rung in this ladder, and it is the greatest thing God can give us, for He Himself is love. And it is the greatest thing we can give to God, for in it we give ourselves and carry with it all that is ours.

Love is the crowning grace of humanity, the holiest right of the soul, the golden link that binds us to duty and truth, and it is the redeeming principle that reconciles the heart to life. It is at this stage on the ladder of life that you hear men say, "I have opened my mouth to the Lord and I cannot turn back." For love never faileth.

CONCLUSION

We are born for higher destiny than earth.
For there is a realm where the rainbow never fades,
where the stars will spread before us like islands that slumber on the ocean,
where the ones that pass on before us here like shadows will remain in our presence forever,
There will be no wearisome nights there, no sorrowful days, no breaches of friendship,
no sad separation, no bitter regrets, no tears, no heartaches,
no death nor crying for the former things are passed away.

Jacob got on his ladder and it carried him through all of his troubles and finally to heaven. We have loved ones who have gone up this ladder and today they are watching us as we climb. As for me, I shall stay on the ladder until I get home and hear my Jesus say, "Well done, good and faithful servant" (Matthew 25:21).

THE SOURCE OF AN ABUNDANT AND LASTING SATISFACTION

"How excellent is thy loving-kindness, oh God! Therefore, the children of men put their trust under the shadow of thy wings. They shall be abundantly satisfied with the fatness of thy house; and thou shall make them drink of the river of thy pleasure" (Psalm 36:6-7).

Satisfaction is something all seek and would love to possess. But this world with all it has to offer has failed to give to its inhabitants true and lasting satisfaction. Everywhere we see humanity (apart from God) rushing, seeking, asking, knocking, and pleading for the assurance of a better, more peaceful, happy, and a more abiding life.

Some hope to find satisfaction in culture or refinement. Some seek it in the possession of this world's goods, while others endeavor to secure it by surrounding themselves with the pleasures of this world. All of these hewn out cisterns fail to hold water that will give lasting satisfaction. And when men have drunk from these wells of the world until they become mentally intoxicated, *still* there is a craving for *something new, better, and more substantial and more abiding.*

In our text from Psalm 36, the psalmist seemed to have summed up the desire of the human family, and pointed man to the source from which he may receive abundant and lasting satisfaction.

Point One

God is the source of this abundant and lasting satisfaction.

"How excellent is thy loving-kindness, oh God!"

This name, the derivation of which is uncertain, we give to that eternal, infinite, perfect, and incomprehensible being we call God. The Creator of the worlds and all things therein. He it is who governs all things by His almighty power and wisdom.

The Bible assumes and exerts the existence of this infinite one by saying, "In the beginning God *created.*" In the interim God preserves and keeps. And when time shall exchange with eternity, this being will still be God.

The Bible is the most illustrious proof of His existence as well as our chief instructor as to His will and nature. It puts a voice into the lips of creation and not only revealed God in His works, but illustrates His way in providence, displays the glory of His character, and brings man into a true and saving communion with God.

He is revealed to us as a spirit, *the only being from everlasting to everlasting.* By nature, [He is] underived, infinite, perfect, and unchangeable in His power, wisdom, omniscience, omnipresence, justice, holiness, truth, goodness, and mercy.

He is the source and ruler of *all* beings and things, foreknows and predetermines all events in nature as well as in man. For "every good gift and every perfect gift cometh from the Father of light, with whom there is no variableness nor shadow of turning" (James 1:17).

This is He who has satisfied the souls of men struggling through life's wilderness. He replied to Moses when he asked His name, "I am that I am" (Exodus 3:14), which denoted I am who I am or I am what I am. In either case the expression implies the eternal existence of Jehovah and his incomprehensible nature. For, in his own way, God is whatever his people need him to be. To Moses he would be a tongue that could speak *even in a king's palace*. For Israel in the wilderness—bread. For Hagar, he was a well of water. For Abraham, a sacrifice. For Joshua, a captain. He was oil for a poor widow. A shield for David and a present help in trouble. He was a key for Paul and Silas. To the Christian, he is a *Rock* in a wearied land, a bridge in deep water, a friend in trouble.

Point Two

The church is the outlet for this abundant and lasting satisfaction.

"They shall be abundantly satisfied with the fatness of thy house and thou shall make them drink of the rivers of thy pleasure."

Let us thank God that this river is not like the "Dead Sea" that receives all and lets nothing out. But our God has an outlet through which flows those blessings, which makes glad and satisfies the hearts of true believers.

This outlet is the Church that Jesus came to earth to establish. "A company of baptized believers associated together by covenant with Jesus Christ. . . Christ died to redeem it and got up out of the grave to justify."

Say what you may about the church, she is still the "light of the world." It is still "the city set on a hill." She is still "the salt of the earth." From her gates thousands, yea, millions have gone into the Kingdom and a like number are on the way while others will be coming this way when we shall cease to exist.

Yes, the members *of the church* shall be satisfied because in him they find *love* and *kindness*. "I have loved thee" says God to Ephraim, "with an everlasting love" (Jeremiah 31:3). "God so loved the world" (John 3:16). Here is not a love that charms the ear and cheats the soul but real substantial favor from God.

They shall be satisfied because they are permitted to drink from the river of God's pleasure: "He that believeth on me out of his soul shall flow rivers [of living water]" (John 7:38).

They shall be satisfied because "in thy light shall we see light" (Psalm 36:9).

Here is a light that has shone and will continue to shine, a power house that does not fail. It showed Daniel how to go into a den of lions and be satisfied. It showed the Hebrew boys a place in the flames where the heat had been extracted. By it, Elisha saw a host that more than equaled his enemies. Stephen could see heaven while being stoned. By this light, Paul saw a "house not made with hands" (2 Corinthians 5:1). It is by this light that every child of God is marching onward to that celestial city!

Let us pray!

THE CHURCH AT SATAN'S HEADQUARTERS

"And unto the angel of the church at Pergamos write; "These things saith he which hath the sharp sword with two edges; I know thy works and where thou dwellest, even where Satan's seat is: and thou holdest fast my name, and hath not denied my faith. . ." (Revelation 2:12-17).

As is seen throughout these messages to the seven churches in Asia, there is one truth that holds with them all, as well as with the Church today: Any real living and conquering Christian or church will meet with opposition.

In the days of the patriarchs, Satan is seen "roving up and down in the earth, seeking whom he may devour." But here in the Revelation, it seems that he has established himself is some particular locality where, with his angels, he is carrying out his evil designs, which causes much concern to those interested in the advancement of the Kingdom of Jesus Christ.

Let us observe to whom this letter was sent—the church at Pergamum. Whether this was a city raised from the ruins of old Troy or another of the same name is neither certain or relevant. It was a place where Christ had called and constituted a church by the preaching of the gospel.

It will also be observed that, in several titles that Christ prefixed to these churches, there is something suited to the individual state of each and all of them. To the drowsy and declining congregation of Ephesus, he speaks to them as one "who holds the stars in his right hand, walking amidst the candlesticks." And to the church at Smyrna, discouraged because of its poverty-stricken condition says He, "I know thy works, tribulation and poverty, but thou art rich." And now, to the church at Pergamos, infested with men of corrupt morals, using their influence to blight the minds of those in harmony with Christ's program, He informs them that He stands ready to fight against them with a two-edged sword.

The word of God is a sword. It is a weapon used as both offensive and defensive, and it is in the hands of God who is able to slay both sin and the sinner. It is a sharp sword, and no heart is so hard but what this sword can penetrate, and no knot is so tightly tied but what this sword can untie. It is a sword with two edges, which turns and cuts every way, and there is no way of escaping it. Whether we turn right or left, backward or forward, up or down, in or out, there is a sword that turns every way to keep the way to the tree of life.

It makes no difference how much or little a man knows, who he sees or what he believes, the flaming sword with its double edge will find its man.

Let us thank God that such an instrument is provided, for how would the Church be able to cope with the satanic wiles at Satan's headquarters were it not for gospel of Jesus Christ.

Point One

The church at Satan's headquarters must do its work.

It is "where Satan's seat is." The works of God's servants are best accepted and known when the condition under which they do their work is taken into consideration. The Lord takes notice of all disadvantages, in opportunities, handicaps, temptations, privations, and hindrances prevailing in the place where we are called upon to serve.

He observes all discouragements, perplexities, ignorance, and downright oppositions, and says to his servants, "I know where thou dwellest." Brethren, don't lose heart if your congregation fails to succeed as others do. Maybe you are closer to the headquarters [of the evil one].

Though we be near Satan's seat, we shouldn't become alarmed, excited, and by negligence to Christian duty allow Satan to reign at ease even though he be at his capitol. But instead, we should use all of our energy to disarm and disband the satanic forces that God's kingdom may come in its stead.

And let us not lose heart because Satan shoots at us, for his arrow cannot reach the heart if Christ controls the bow. Again, the church or Christian that no one opposes is most certainly to be trifling and useless about the King's business.

This, I am sure, is the explanation of those shocking words that fall from the lips of Jesus, "Woe be unto you when all men speak well of you" (Luke 6:26). When sinful and evil men, gangsters and the underworld, hypocrites and unregenerate men, backsliders and reprobates are all singing our praises, *it's time to check out our Christianity.*

The Christianity that Jesus puts His approval on is a positive force in the world. It stands for economic, social, and religious righteousness. And in doing so, we are certain to arouse the antagonism of the forces of evil. For this world is no friend to grace and we must not accept its goodwill.

Point Two

The faults and shortcomings of the Church at Satan's headquarters.

"I have a few things against you."

After listening to where this church dwelt and the sufferings they encountered, one may be surprised to know that they were short in their functioning, but let us thank God that they (as well as we) were not as bad as the picture painted. God had only a few things against them.

If we listen to the accusations of the devil, everything is wrong with the church. If we take to heart all we hear in the streets, everybody is wrong in the church. If we look at the picture released from hell, everything is dark and dismal in the church. But this church had only a *few things* that displeased the Lord. And allow me to pause long enough to let you know that *the Lord is the only One we are trying to please.*

For the benefit of those who stand on the corner and criticize the church, we should like to borrow from Dr. William L. Ransom of Richmond, Virginia, in his book, *What's Right with the Church.* He tells us and substantiates it by the Word of God that "the church has the right origin. Founded by Jesus himself and grounded upon the faith of the faithful, and will continue to function when all of her critics are smoldering in the unquenchable fires of hell." Jesus said, "I will build My church" (Matthew 16:18).

The Church has the right constitution, the Word of God, which was written by men divinely inspired, and is a perfect treasure of heavenly instruction. It has God for its author, salvation for its end, and truth without any mixture of error for its matter. The Church has the right requirement for its membership. "You must be born again" (John 3:7).

The Church has the right standard for leadership. Whatever the devil may do to him, he is God's man, and the world cannot be saved until he arrives with the good news of the gospel: "How can they hear without a preacher" (Romans 10:14).

The Church is on the right journey and she has the right of way. Her saints may be banished on lonely islands, her leaders may be stoned while others have their heads severed from their bodies, but God's church goes on from victory to victory. Her founder is still walking among the seven candlesticks holding the angels of the church in His hand.

Therefore, we pause like Moses on the way to the Promised Land and say, "Cease fighting the church, and come thou with us, and we will do thee good."

The old Church shall march on until our feet strike the bright land of an unclouded day when Jesus, who came to the world to redeem her, Jesus, who died to save her, Jesus, who got up from a grave to justify her, will serve us.

Point Three

The church at Satan's headquarters is commended for her faithfulness amidst difficult situations.

"Thou boldest fast my name and hath not denied the faith."

Certainly this church and its leaders need to be commended, for anyone can serve when the sun is shining. Anyone can serve when everyone around you is singing your praises. But wait until you are criticized for the good you do. Wait until you have become wounded in the house of your friends. What about it when you must go into the furnace or on a lonely island?

There were two very noteworthy characteristics that were instrumental in helping this church to stand against adversity. And it would be well for the church today to embrace them for if we expect to stand, and that is that *we must have something to hold on to.*

It's fine to have friends who we can go to with our problems, but friends will let you down. Its pleasant to have people singing your praises, but people today would be glad to be at your funeral. It's good to have a reliable bank account to depend on when times are lean, but if you expect to stand against Satan you will need something within.

What would you recommend? Though, this which I am recommending has been the Rock of Ages, yet I know of nothing better——His name is Jesus.

- Hold on to Jesus, for by Him worlds were spoken into existence.
- Hold on to Jesus, for He hung worlds on His word, and they are still there.
- Hold on to Jesus, for all power is in His hand.
- Hold on to Jesus, for at His name every knee shall bow.
- Hold on to Jesus, for He is a battle-axe during war, a friend in time of trouble, shelter in the time of storm, doctor in the sick room, dying bed maker, mind regulator.

Yes, take the name of Jesus with you, child of sorrow and of woe, on your job, in the laundry, on the streets, in the morning, at evening when you retire

Point Four

The encouragement Jesus gives to the faithful church at Satan's headquarters.

"To him that overcometh will I give to eat of the hidden manna, and will give him a white stone."

Thanks be to God that those who have made up their minds to persevere to the end, Christ has never left them without some hope of assurance, some light to guide them through, some sure support against despair.

You ask what is it that is here offered? It is hidden manna, the influence and the Spirit of Christ coming down into the very soul of the saints. It is that which permits the pilgrims to taste something of how the angels live in heaven.

This is hidden from the world: money can't buy it, refinement can't procure it, knowledge cannot impart it. To gain this manna, one must leave Egypt, they must be born again.

Jesus died on Calvary to free us from Satan's headquarters. He got up from the grave and gave to us our passport. No wonder the saints can sing, "I will overcome someday. . ."

Church, fight on and hold on to God's unchanging hand. After a while, we will pack up and move out from Satan's headquarters. For one day, John saw a number moving from Satan's headquarters: a hundred and forty-four thousand and a number which no man could number. They had washed their robes and made them white in the blood of the Lamb. If I never speak to you again here, I'll pick you up on the boardwalk in glory.

THE VOYAGES OF LIFE

"And straightway Jesus constrained his disciples to get into a ship, and to go before him unto the other side, while he sent the multitudes away. And when he had sent the multitudes away, he went up into a mountain apart to pray: and when the evening was come, he was there alone. But the ship was now in the midst of the sea, tossed with waves: for the wind was contrary" (Matthew 14:22-24).

"Unto the other side" are watch words of faith breaking through all narrow boundaries, watch words of love overcoming all selfishness, watch words of courage facing all danger. Christ is saying to us today as He did to His original followers: Get into the ship of time and go before me unto the other side.

He is ever calling for us to pass over some line into new fields of experience, privileges, duties, conflicts, and joys. He commands it of the penitent when He invites them to become His disciples. He wants them to cut loose from the world, from sin and all of its dead past to arise and go with Him to the better life that lies beyond. He extends the call to His saints as they struggle with the problems of this life. And while before them rolls the sea, dark and full of tenor, they can rest assured that on the other side, glory awaits.

The verses preceding the text relates the story of one of Christ's miracles when he fed the 5,000 men besides women and children from five loaves and a few fish, and how the disciples had taken a basket of food for each of themselves.

Because of this miracle, the people were conspiring to make him a king and the disciples were likely to join their attempt. Therefore, Jesus constrained them to take the ship to the other side of the lake, to encounter the storm, the wind, and the waves. For Jesus knew, and we will find out if we keep on living, that people who sing your praise today would be glad to sing it at your funeral tomorrow.

Also they were to learn this lesson, which all of Christ's followers should observe, that, after every calm, after every manifestation of the power of the Holy Ghost, after every glorious experience, there will be storms to face, and waves and winds to encounter.

Christ would have us know that the path which leads to any height does not always lie among flowers, but often among thorns and thistles. And those who travel this path may find their feet pierced with thorns. It is too often our wish to be lifted by some supernatural power and carried by the praise of men into the very presence of God. But Jesus would have us know that if we would be fortunate enough to achieve the heights, we will not fall once we are up there. There will be storms, winds, and waves to encounter.

He who walks this path may faint in the dismal valley and experience their rest at midnight on desert sand. But whatever the price we are called to pay, we must meet Christ on the "other side." Behind this symbolism, let us observe some worthwhile lessons that are essential as we launch forth on this voyage of life.

How unexpected and what a disheartening change it must have been for the disciples. They had just experienced a calm setting of the sun, a sober evening clothing the quiet vale.

Point One

The unexpected changes and circumstances of life's voyage.

They saw the rose and purple transfiguration of the mountaintop. They experienced the peaceful rocking of the slumbering waves, and the joy of feeding the five thousand with the loaves multiplying in their hands. But then they found themselves in a struggle, fighting against the waves, peering through the darkness, and rowing against the wind.

What a picture of life this narrative reveals of all who have launched forth to meet Jesus! What unexpected changes often meet us on our journey, causing labor, pain, heartaches, burdens, and sorrow. Often the loom of life has been arranged to produce a pattern to our liking and, for a while, the swift shuttle of time flying through the warp of our affairs weaves a fabric both pleasant to ourselves and others.

But then, an unseen hand silently shifts the machinery of life, producing strange and unrecognized experiences. The friend we had trusted proves unfriendly, the good we have done for others becomes unappreciated, the sacrifices we have made seem unrecognized, the toils and problems encountered produced the unexpected changes or vicissitudes of life.

Observe, here is that which adds heat to the flame. When you are where Jesus told you to go and doing what He told you to do, and yet the storms arise, the wind blows, and the waves dash high. But don't lose heart, the disciples encountered the same on their voyage. And none are such spoiled children of fortune as to be able to make the journey without some storms. This experience reveals a truth that has been observed in all Christendom:

- Abraham had his Mount Moriah, Job had his land of Ur,
- Daniel [had his relocation] to Babylon, Paul and Silas had their jail in Philippi, and
- John had his isle of Patmos.

Yes, we too are tossed and driven on a restless sea of time; somber skies and howling tempest oft follow a bright sunshine. Yes, temptations and hidden snares often take us unawares, and our hearts are made to bleed for a thoughtless word or deed; and we wonder why the test when we try to do our best.

Yes, brethren, these unexpected vicissitudes or crucial circumstances will come while you are on life's voyage, but take courage from God's Word: "Think it not strange concerning the fiery trials which is to try you, as though some strange thing was happening to you, but rejoice in as much as ye are partakers of Christ's sufferings" (1 Peter 4:12); "For if we suffer with him, we shall also reign with him" (2 Timothy 2:12) cried Paul; and "I reckon that the suffering of this world is not worthy to be compared with the glory which shall be revealed on the other side" (Romans 8:18).

Point Two

In the hour of our deepest need, Christ will come to our rescue.

"In the fourth watch of the night, Jesus went to them."

Here is an encouraging note that gives strength to the pilgrim as he journeys to the other side—"Jesus will come." It is of the goodness of Christ that He comes to us. He is cognizant of our case, possessing a knowledge of our struggles, and He is concerned about our welfare. J. Lincoln Hall asked these questions in the famous song:

"Does Jesus care when my heart is pained
too deeply for mirth or song,
As the burdens press and cares distress,
and the way grows weary and long?
Does Jesus care when my way is dark,
with a nameless dread and fear?
As the daylight fades into deep night shade,
does he care enough to be near?
Oh yes! He cares, I know he cares; his heart is touched with my grief,
when the days are weary, the long night dreary."

The disciples seemed alone out there on a stormy sea, and I imagine they asked themselves the same questions that Hall asked. But up yonder in some hidden cleft of the hills, their Master looked down on the weltering storm and prayed for them that their faith would not fail. Then when the need was the sorest, when hope had failed, He came across the waves, making their surges His pavement and using all oppositions as a means of His approach.

Yes, when God wills, the mad rushing waters of a Red Sea will form themselves into a wall allowing Israel to cross over on dry land. When God wills, loaves of bread will float from heaven's bakery to feed the hungry Israelites in the wilderness. When God wills, Jericho's walls will fold and crumble like a clod of dirt beneath chariot wheels. When God wills, the sun will stand still while we fight our battles. When God wills, the heat will disappear from the flames, proud waves will cease to roll, the wind will fold itself into closets of calmness, burdens will roll away, and sunshine will take the place of shadows.

He will come, says Charles H. Gabriel,

"Just when I need him Jesus is near,
Just when I falter, just when I fear,
Ready to help me, ready to cheer
Just when I need him most.
Just when I need him, He is my all,
Answering when upon Him I call;
Tenderly watching lest I should fall,
Just when I need Him most."

Point Three

The consolation that Christ's presence brings to His people on life's able voyage.

"Be not afraid, it is I."

Though it was dark, stormy, and dangerous, these words did something for the disciples, and we too shall hear these consoling words if we hold on. This jet age in which we live has no answer for the deep cry of the soul. This space and missile age cannot be depended upon for security. We need someone who can save us from the circumstances we find ourselves in.

"Who would you recommend, preacher?" I want to thank God that, having had many years of experience on this voyage of life, I feel qualified to make a recommendation. For I have seen the lightning flashing and I have heard the thunder roll. I have been in storms. I have had waves to beat upon me and the wind has blown on me.

But I heard somebody say, "Be not afraid." And I would like to recommend that person to you. It is Jesus:

- Who rolls the orbs of heaven with His hands, who fixes the earth with His foot;
- Who guides all creatures with His eye and refreshes them with His influence;
- He makes the powers of hell to shake with His terror, and binds the devil with His word. Who is the challenge to the proud dreams of empires;
- Who turns the world upside down and the upside down turns out to be the right side up.

I recommend Jesus:

- The Son of righteousness, whose name blossoms on every page of history like a flower of a thousand spring times.
- Whose name sounds down through the centuries like the music of a million choirs. Who died on Calvary and by His death saved a perishing world.
- Who arose from the grave on Sunday morning with all power in His hand.
- Who came back to visit John on Patmos saying, "I am He that was dead and is alive forevermore."
- Who chartered a plane from Olivet and stopped it in mid-air to shout back these encouraging words to His church, "Lo, I am with you always."

He brought His disciples over to the other side and He will bring us over.

TO WHOM SHALL WE GO?

"Then Simon Peter answered him, 'Lord; to whom shall we go? Thou hast the words of eternal life. And we believe and are sure that Thou art the Christ, the Son of the living God'"
(John 6:68-69).

INTRODUCTION

Last Sunday, we closed out our calendar year and we are grateful to God, who has brought us through that year, as well as the many that have gone before. As we come to the beginning of this church year, we find ourselves faced with the same situation that the followers of Christ experienced hundreds of years ago, when we are called upon to decide which course in life we will take.

There are striking incidents in the life of Jesus that compare to our situation today—when people are dissatisfied with life as it is, and are constantly in search of different experiments that will give them a better life There is nothing wrong with such experimentations, for none should maintain the "status quo" position in Christian living, but search for avenues that lead to higher heights, wider horizons, and deeper depths in Christ. When Christ came to this world, He seemed to have had the answer to the wants and desires of the people. Eagerly they turned to him by the thousands.

But soon they discovered that He was not the person for their purpose. They sought earthly advantages but instead heavenly blessings were offered to them. They expected one who would restore the kingdom of David, and the Kingdom of heaven was the highlight of His messages. They invited Jesus to take a hand in legal matters such as rightly dividing inheritance between brothers and was informed that men should lay up for themselves treasures in heaven. They came to Him by the thousands looking for loaves such as they had been fed with in the wilderness and were informed, "I am the bread of life, which, if a man eat, he will hunger no more" (John 6:35).

Then, as it is now, Christ's method did not meet their approval. To them, it did not seem forceful enough, so many went back and walked no more with Him. It was here that Jesus turned to them who knew Him best; those who He called from fishing boats, collecting taxes and other ordinary occupations of life, saying, "Will ye also go away?" (John 6:67). Thanks be to God that Peter was there with the answer to this all-important question. The answer was strong and confident. And let us hope that before the close of this message that all of us might come to the same conclusion as confidently as Peter did. That Jesus only "has the words of eternal life" (John 6:68).

To assist us in reaching this conclusion,

Point One

Let us look at the question itself.

"To whom shall we go?" What alternatives are there open to us? What can substitute for Christ? Which path seems to lead to a better life?

If we thoroughly consider these questions, analyzing them for their worth and value, we will have to decide with Peter that only Jesus can save the day for us. What Peter wanted, and what we need is, first of all, someone who can raise us above our circumstances. Multitudes of the human family are so placed as to be in perpetual and unfavorable circumstances. The odds, disappointments, and disillusions, the dullness of life's routine and the dreary unmarked rounds of duty, the seeing no end and no prospect for any brighter future, the being placed where we had rather not be, and the hopelessness of any change from it, are all against us.

All of these are common experiences, and it is a want of ours to find someone who has the ability and the willingness to master the situation: "To whom shall we go?" (John 6:68).

Some are trying escapism, trying to ignore these situations by plunging into a continual round of business and pleasure or, as some put it, "letting the world go by." They hope by escapism to silence the voices within their soul. But one trouble with escapism is that it leaves the world and conditions just as they are. When we pass up problems, chaos, tragedy, and unwholesomeness continue to become worse. God has so made this world with its inhabitants, that he will do nothing for us until we are ready to let Him do something *through* us.

Another difficulty about living an escapist's life is that we cannot continue to escape from ourselves. However full and exciting we may make our days, somewhere and sometime, life has a way of catching up with us. This "catching up with us" will present the yearning for a better richer, fuller, and a more complete life. This yearning may come because of sudden shock, sorrow, sickness, uneasiness, disappointments, and bereavements. But whatever the occasion may be, we are made to realize that no man can run away from his own self, or from God.

Some try changing environments. This is what many people have relied on to lead them to a better life. But to their dismay, they have found environment in itself cannot make us what we ought to be. In our social order and life, men imagine that by some rearrangement of external condition, a new and better life will be experienced. So they yearn for a change of environment: another job, finer homes, higher salary. All of these are good and we urge you to secure them and as many other of this world's blessings as you can, and do so honestly. But while rearranging external conditions, we must not forget that the spirit needs changing with the structure of society. For to undertake the one without the other is, in the end, to be as we were. I like the poem that reads,

Do not wait until some deed of greatness you may do,
Do not wait to spread your light afar
To the many duties ever near you, now be true
Brighten the corner where you are.

Some hope to find the better and richer life by being a moralist. We must admit that by living a good moral life, one moves closer to the needs of our day and age. For it is by moral recovery and ethical revival, by advancing moral ideas and standards, that we make better societies and communities. But may we admonish you, without condoning immorality, that there are many good moral individuals who we know and associate with daily, but who, for the lack of salvation, are on their way to damnation.

The history of Christianity reveals the fact of many that were not so good morally but, deep down within, they had someone who saved the day, and brought them out more than conquerors. We are mindful of the saying of Solomon, "That a good name is better than fine gold" (Proverbs 22:1).

Now consider what a good name is. In Acts 11:26, you will find the good name that Solomon spoke of: "The disciples were called Christians first at Antioch." Many biblical characters would not measure up to the standard of our modern day moralists. But they had Christ and He made up the shortage. So are you looking for a better, richer, deeper, and more dedicated life? Then, let us observe the answer of Christianity,

Point Two

None but Christ can satisfy.

"Thou hast the words of eternal life" (John 6:68).

Herein lies the answer. Here is the path we have been looking for. Here is the one that the world needs to find. Our longing for a better life is not denied us. Although escapism, environmental changes, and the way of the moralist are all unable to furnish a remedy, the place of renewal and recovery is where it has always been: "Thou hast the words of eternal life."

There is only one force in all the world that can change the moral tone and atmosphere of a nation. There is only one power in the whole universe which can take any of us and all of us as we are and make us what we should be. That power is the gospel of the Son of God.

CONCLUSION

A roll call of the best men who have lived and are living today acknowledges that only Jesus has the words of eternal life. Recall the philosophers, among whom are Baker, Locke, and Johnson. The astronomers, among whom were Kepler, Cooper, and Newton. The scientists, among whom are Boncroft, Wilbur, and Green. The discoverers, among whom were Livingston, Raleigh, and Stanley. All of these took time from their busy schedules to acknowledge that only Jesus has the words of eternal life.

Let the roll call of patriarchs speak in their order:

- Abraham said, "The Lord will provide the sacrifice" (Genesis 22:8).
- Jacob, "Unto him shall the gathering of the people be" (Genesis 49:10).
- Job declared, "I will wait until my change comes" (Job 14:14).

The prophets were listed on the roll in the persons of

- Isaiah, who said, "Unto us a child is born, and unto us a son is given, and the government shall be upon his shoulders, and his name shall be called wonderful, counselor, the mighty God, the everlasting Father, the Prince of Peace" (Isaiah 9:6).
- Ezekiel says of him, "He is a wheel in the middle of a wheel" (Ezekiel 1:16).

Daniel observed, "He is a stone cut out of the mountain without hands" (Daniel 2:45). Listed among the poets' roll, we have David who revealed, "The Lord is my shepherd, I shall not want" (Psalm 23:1). Call the roll of believers and they will tell you that He is a friend in trouble; a rock in a weary land; bread when you're hungry; water when you're thirsty; and light in darkness.

He is the one who calms our fears,
bids our sorrows cease.
He's the music to the sinner's ear,

and life, and health and peace.

He breaks the power to reigning sin,
and sets the prisoners free,
His blood can make the foulest clean,
His blood availed for me.

And most important, finally, He is our way to that celestial city which has a foundation whose builder and maker is God. Amen.

SHARING THE RESURRECTION

"Marvel not at this: for the hour is coming, in which all that are in the grave shall hear his voice, and shall come forth; they that have done good, unto the resurrection of life; and they that have done evil, to the resurrection of damnation" (John 5:28-29).

The earth has been arched with graves—the last lodging place of all mortals—and the bottom of the ocean is paved with bones of men. Life was at first confined to one couple. But how soon and how wide did it spread. How inconceivably numerous are the sons of Adam! How many are the different nations on our globe containing millions of humans, even in one generation! And how many generations have succeeded one another in the course of nearly six thousand years.

Let your imagination call up this vast army. Children that merely lighted upon our globe and then winged their flight into an unknown world. The gray-headed that had a long journey through life. The blooming youth and the middle-aged. Let them pass in review before us from all countries and from all ages, and we will see how vast and astonishing this multitude is.

If the posterity of one man, Abraham, by one son was, according to the divine promise, as innumerable as the stars of the heaven or the sand of the seashore, what counting can compute the multitude that have sprung from all the patriarchs and the succeeding generations! But what has become of them all? Alas, they are turned into earth, their original element. They are imprisoned in the grave, except the present generation, and we are dropping one after another in quick succession.

The greatest number of humans, without doubt, are sleeping beneath the ground. There lies beauty moldering into dust furnishing food for the vilest worms. There lie the mighty giants, the heroes, and the conquerors. The Samsons, the Alexanders, and the Caesars of the world. There lie the wise and the learned as well as the ignorant and the foolish. There lie those who we once conversed with, some who were our best friends, our companions, our fathers and mothers, our sisters and brothers.

But shall they lie there always? Shall this body, this curious workmanship of heaven, so wonderfully and fearfully made, lie in ruins and never be repaired? Shall the wide extended valleys of dry bones never live again? The answer to these vital questions is found in the words of Jesus, the author of the text, "The hour is coming when all that are in the grave shall hear the voice of the Son of God, and shall come forth" (John 5:25).

Point One

All must hear His voice.

This is the voice of Jesus Christ of Nazareth who got up from a grave Himself more than two thousand years ago. He issued invitations to teeming millions who would follow. He says,

- "Come unto me, all ye that labor and are heavy laden, and I will give you rest" (Matthew 11:28-29).

- "I am the way, the truth, and the life, no man cometh unto the Father but by me" (John 14:6).
- "I go to prepare a place for you, that where I am, there ye may be also" (John 14:2-3).

Today, the voice of mercy calls, reason pleads, and conscience warns, but millions will not hear. Here, however, is a voice that the billions, both upon and under the earth, must hear. None shall be able to stop his ears or ignore the voice. Infants and giants, kings and subjects, high and low—all ranks, all ages of mankind shall hear the call.

The living shall start and be changed and the dead shall rise at the sound. The dust that was once alive and formed a human body, whether it flies in the air, floats on the ocean, or vegetates on earth, shall hear the voice. For wherever the fragments of the human frame are scattered, they shall be revived by the penetrating voice. To the grave the call will be, "Arise ye dead and come to judgment, to heaven, ye spirits of just men made perfect" (see Hebrews 12:23).

Point Two

They shall come forth.

Many hear the voice of Jesus pleading today, but they refuse to obey it. They want more time to enjoy the pleasures of this world. Many say, "I hear the voice, but I want to get right before I come. I don't want to be a hypocrite." Others give varied excuses and reasons for failing to heed the call of Christ.

But when Christ calls on that final day, all *must* come. Visualize, if you will, and hear the earth heaving, tombs bursting, graves opening, the noise and shaking among the bones. The dust is alive and in motion as this vast army is working its way through. If there were any to ask them whither they were bound, they would answer, "I must go to judgment to stand on trial."

The ruins of human bodies may be scattered far and wide and may have passed through many surprising transformations—a limb in one country and the other in another. The head may be here and the trunk yonder with oceans rolling between. Multitudes may have sunken into a watery grave and been swallowed up by the monsters of the sea. There may be those who have been devoured by beasts or birds of prey, while others have moldered into dust, this dust having been blown about by wind or washed away by water. Or it may have petrified into stone and then buried into bricks to form dwellings for their posterity.

But through all of these transformations and changes, not a particle that is essential to a human body has been lost. The omnipotent, omnipresent, all-wise and eternal God knows how to collect, distinguish, and compound all of those scattered and mangled bodies of the human family: "Lord," cried Moses, "Thou hast been our dwelling place through all generations" (Psalm 90:1).

Point Three

The grounds of distinction in the final state of man.

There has always been a distinction among men. Either you are good or bad, right or wrong—there is no middle ground. Says Jesus, "You are either with me or against me" (see Luke

11:23). On which side are you?

What are some of the benefits of being on the side of righteousness? There are many. Many to be observed here and now, but in order to stay with the text, we shall discuss the two found therein. And for the sake of glorified terms, we shall reverse the order of this part of the text.

A. They who have done evil shall experience the resurrection of damnation.

How, and what language shall I use, to describe the case of the evil doers as their bodies burst from the grave but to use the miserable spectacles of horror and deformity? Visualize, if you will, the millions of gloomy ghosts rising like pillars of smoke from the bottomless pit. With what reluctance and anguish do they reenter their old habitation! What a dreadful meeting! What a shocking salutation!

"O thou accursed body, the system of deformity and terror. In thee I once sinned, by thee I was ensnared, debased and ruined. To gratify thy vile lusts and appetites, I neglected my own immortal interest, degraded my native dignity, and have made myself miserable forever.

"Once I received sensations of pleasure from thee, but now thou art transformed into an engine of torture. No more through thine eyes shall I behold the cheerful light of the day, and the beautiful prospects of nature, but the thick gloom of hell, grim and ghastly, while Heaven will be at an impassable distance and all the horrid sights of woe in the infernal regions.

"No more shall thine ears charm me with the harmony of sound, but terrify and distress me with the echo of eternal groans, and the thunder of the Almighty's vengeance. Thy tongue which I employed in mirth and jest and song, shall utter groans, complaints, blasphemy and torture forever. Thy feet that once walked in the flowery enchanted path of sin must now walk on the burning soil of hell."

However urgent the petition of the evil doer, the reluctant soul must enter its prison from whence it shall never more be dismissed. For the Scripture says, "These shall go away into everlasting darkness" (Matthew 25:46).

But, let us thank God that there is a brighter side to this picture.

B. They that have done good shall experience the resurrection of life.

Those who have given their lives, their time, and their talents will hear Jehovah say to them, "Well done, good and faithful servant" (Matthew 25:23).

What a difference in the final state of men! With what joy will the spirits of the righteous welcome their old companions from their long sleep in the dust and congratulate their glorious resurrection! How they will rejoice to reenter their old habitation, now so completely repaired and highly improved.

Those bodies which were once their encumbrance, their languish, their temptation, once frail and mortal—tainted with the seed of sin—are now their assistants and co-partners in the business of heaven. Now vigorous, incorruptible, and immortal, free from all corrupt mixtures and shining in all the beauty of perfect holiness.

In these bodies they once served God with honest, though feeble efforts, conflicted with sin and temptations, passing through all the united trials and hardships of this life.

But now they are united for more exalted purposes. The lungs that once heaved with penitential sighs and groans shall now shout forth their joy and praise to God their Savior. The heart that was once broken with sorrow shall be bound up forever and overflow with immortal pleasure. Their eyes that once ran with tears shall now behold the King in His beauty, along with the glories of heaven, for God shall wipe away all tears from their eyes.

What assurance do we have of this glorious triumph? Jesus gave it to John on the isle of Patmos: "I am he that was dead, but now, I am alive forevermore, and because I live, ye shall live also" (Revelation 1:18). As the song tells us,

I serve a risen Savior, he's in the world today,
I know that he is living whatever men may say;
I see his hand of mercy, I hear his voice of cheer
And just the time I need him he's always near

In all the world around me I see his loving care,
And though my heart grows weary I never will despair,
I know that he is leading through all the stormy blast,
The day of his appearing will come at last.

Rejoice, rejoice, oh Christian, lift up your voice and sing
Eternal hallelujah to Jesus Christ, the king;
The hope of all who seek him, the help of all who find,
None other is so loving, so good and kind.

He lives! He lives! Christ Jesus lives today.
He walks with me and talks with me
Along the narrow way.
He lives! He lives! Salvation to impart,
You ask me, "How I know he lives?"
He lives within my heart.

STRIKING IT RICH

"And you hath he quickened, who were dead in trespasses and sins;
wherein in time past ye walked according to the course of this world...
But God, who is rich in mercy, for his great love wherewith he loved us,
even when we were dead in sins, hath quickened us together with Christ" (Ephesians 2:1-5).

We are certain that this theme is one that all are familiar with, for its almost impossible to turn on the television without observing and viewing this program, "Strike It Rich." Not only is it a familiar one but it is one that all would like to become - recipients of the vast and generous fortunes that are handed out on these programs.

Many of us cannot be privileged to appear on and compete with other contestants on our radio and television, but here is a program in which all can appear and one in which you will be sure to win: "For God who is rich in mercy, by his great love, hath quickened us together with Christ" (Ephesians 2:5). What greater riches could one achieve? What greater benefits could be derived from any source than to be quickened together with Christ?

On the physical "Strike It Rich" program, one thing is essentially important—to have some knowledge of the subject in question. And this same principle is true with those who would strike it rich with God. Whatever else we may not know, we must know Him "in whom we have believed."

Point One

Our previous state or condition before we struck it rich.

In order to correctly appreciate present and valuable blessings, it is important to realize what one was before, and by so doing, higher and more worthwhile value will be placed on what we have received. So the Apostle goes on in this chapter to inform the Ephesians and through them, you and I, what we were:

(a) "Dead in trespasses and sins."

All unregenerate souls are dead in trespasses and sins, which signifies all sorts of sin: habitual, and sins of the life and of the heart and mind. And wherever this condition prevails, there is a privation of all spiritual life - being cut off from God, the fountain of life.

(b) How we walked before striking it rich.

We "walked according to the course of this world." Sinners are slaves to Satan for they walk according to him. They conform their lives and actions to the will and pleasure of this usurper. The course and tenor of their lives are according to his suggestion and in compliance with his temptation. They are subject to him and are led captive by him at this will.

(c) The Christ-less condition we are in.

[Before Christ, we are] Gentiles in the flesh and aliens to the commonwealth of Israel and strangers from the covenant promise. In this condition, we recognize ourselves as being without any knowledge of God, without any saving interest in him, or any relation to him. This condition rendered us aliens from the commonwealth of Israel; that is, we did not belong to Christ's church, sharing its worship, ordinances and the peculiar advantages found therein.

(d) Strangers from the covenant of promise.

This covenant is called the covenant of promise because it is made up of the promises of God. It is said there are more than 5,000 of these found in the Bible, giving strength, hope, inspiration, courage, and fortitude to those who are struggling to overcome. "I had fainted," David said, "unless I had hope to see the goodness of the Lord in the land of the living" (Psalm 24:13). Before we struck it rich, we had no hope beyond this life, no promise of God's protective care and no assurance of eternal life in the world to come. How miserable and poor and blind we were before striking it rich.

Point Two

The glorious change wrought in believers since striking it rich.

"But now in Christ Jesus ye who were afar off, are made nigh by the blood of Christ" (Ephesians 2:13).

The narrative reveals that at one time, we were far off from Christ, from His church, His promises, from the Christian hope, far from God Himself, and therefore, like the prodigal son in a far country, far from all that's good. But thanks be to God, we have struck it rich in that we have been brought nigh.

(a) By whom and in what manner were we able to strike it rich?

Negatively: "Not of ourselves." Our faith, our conversation, and our salvation are not the results of our natural abilities, nor any merits of our own. They were not brought to pass by anything done by us: "For by grace are ye saved, through faith, and that not of ourselves, it is the gift of God." (Ephesians 2:8-9). There is no room for any man's boasting of his own ability and power as though he had done anything that might deserve such favors from God.

Positively: God who is rich in mercy and is the Author of this great and glorious change, and His great love is the spring and cause of it: "God so loved the world" (see John 3:16).

Justice respects us apostates (those drifting from righteous principles and ideals) and miserable creatures. But God's eternal love is the fountain from whence all of His mercies proceeds, and that love is a great love and that mercy is a rich mercy—inexpressibly great and inexhaustibly rich.

It was in view of this inexpressibly great love that the poet sang,

> Amazing grace, how sweet the sound,
> That saved a wretch like me;
> I once was lost, but now, I'm found,
> Was blind, but now I see.

Yes, we who were dead are quickened. We are saved from the death of sin and possess a principle of spiritual life implanted in us. Observe that regenerated persons become living souls. They live a life of sanctification. They live not under the law, but under grace. And this spiritual life is the result of our union with Christ. It is "In him that we live, move, and have our being" (Acts 17:28). For, "Because I live", Jesus said, "You shall live also" (see John 6:57).

When God raised Christ from the dead, He did in effect raise up all believers together with Him, He being their common head. And when He placed Christ at His right hand in heavenly places, He advanced and glorified believers in and with Him, causing us to sit together in heavenly places in Christ Jesus.

Point Three

The glorious privilege extended those who have struck it rich.

"[We] are no more strangers and foreigners, but fellow citizens with the saints and of the household of God" (Ephesians 2:19).

The passage reveals the fact that at one time we were aliens and separated from God, and facing a wall that hindered our approach to Him, a disturbance that canceled our peace, but in Christ Jesus we have struck it rich, in that, "He is our peace," the enmity between God and man has been reconciled. He has broken down the wall that hindered our approach. It is no wonder that John could write to the church and say, "Beloved, now are we the sons of God" (1 John 3:2).

Yes, there is enmity between God and sinners, and Christ came to slay that enmity, to break up the quarrel between God and man by reconciling sinners to God. And by his death on the cross, collected them and brought them together, thereby affording free access to God. "

We can come boldly to the throne of grace" (Hebrews 4:16).

Yes, we are no more strangers, but fellow-citizens with the saints and the household of God, which is compared to a city extending privileges to all its citizens; to a house and those who have struck it rich as one of the domestics, one of the family, a child in God's house.

We can come home when we feel like it. We have a key to the apartment. We can relax in the presence of God.

> I'm a child of the king,
> I'm a child of the king,
> With Jesus my Savior,
> I'm a child of the king!

If you have struck it rich you can go home one day and tell the angels to make more room!

PATHWAYS TO POWER

"But what things were gain to me, those I counted loss for Christ. Yea doubtless, and I count all things but loss for the excellency of the knowledge of Christ Jesus my Lord: for whom I have suffered the loss of all things, and do count them but dung, that I may win Christ, And be found in him, not having mine own righteousness, which is of the law, but that which is through the faith of Christ, the righteousness which is of God by faith: That I may know him and the power of his resurrection and the fellowship of his suffering" (Philippians 3:10).

All of us are more or less secretly dissatisfied with ourselves. We long to know God in deeper, sweeter, and a more satisfied way. We are anxious to explore the resources that are ours in Christ. This message is for such Christians who want to reach a place in their spiritual lives where they can be fruitful, exercise more power, and where they can possess more moral and spiritual happiness. Paul, here in these verses, tells us how we can have this satisfaction (vs. 7-9).

If there ever was a time in the history of mankind that we need to know and to find out more about God, if there ever was a time that we need to possess more power to work for God and to vindicate His cause in the world, the time is now.

This power is needful because the devil has unleashed all of his powerful forces against the Church and against the Christian family. And the only way to retaliate against the power of darkness is to possess more of the power of Him who has all power! To wrestle against principalities, we need power from God.

Path One

Some personal knowledge of Jesus.

"That I may know Him."

Whatever else we may not know, here is one thing we must know if we are to succeed in the great work of kingdom building: Know for yourself that you have been born again. We must know it so well that when others don't believe it and say you don't have it, you can still say, "I know in whom I have believed."

It must be admitted that the fathers of yesteryear did not know as much about material things as we know today, but they knew the Lord. And because they knew Him, they could carry on for and are responsible for the monuments of Christian endeavor that are erected in our midst today.

Says one of the fathers, " I don't know why all my children are slain, all my sheep and camels were taken, why all my wealth was taken, why my wife has turned against me, why I am broke out in sores from my head to me feet. But I know that my redeemer liveth" (see Job 19:25). Another said, "I don't know why we were cast into the fire, but I know that our God will deliver." Some of the saints would say, "I know the Lord will make a way somehow."

Path Two

Personal renunciation of the things of the world.

"But what things were gain to me, these I count as loss for Christ."

The Apostle here presents himself as an example of renouncing his privileges as an Israelite and conforming to the wishes and will of God. He had as much to boast of as any Jew and as much as them all.

(1) His birthright privilege

He was not a proselyte but a native Israelite, of the stock of Israel. And he was of the tribe of Benjamin in which the temple stood and which adhered to Judah when all the other tribes revolted. [He was] of the tribe of Benjamin, which was his father's heart, but all this he counted as nothing.

He could boast of his family relations; he was a Hebrew of a Hebrews. None of his ancestors had mixed and mingled with the Gentiles, but this too was nothing.

He could boast of his relation to the church. He had the token of the covenant in his flesh. Circumcised the very day which God had appointed, the eighth day.

He could boast of his blameless conversation, touching the righteousness that is in the Law, blameless.

But all these things he counted loss for Christ. Not only did he count them insufficient to enrich him, but they would certainly impoverish and ruin him if he trusted in them.

My friends, it is an old but true saying. You cannot hold God in one hand and the devil in the other and have power with God. The call to "come out from among them" is still clear and as necessary today as it was when Paul uttered it.

If we would have power with God, we must renounce our righteousness and our goodness and rely on the righteousness and goodness of God.

Path Three

Forgetting the past and making strenuous efforts to advance forward.

"Forgetting those things which are behind and reaching forward to those things which are before, I press toward the mark for the prize of the high calling of God in Christ Jesus."

The devil is no more satisfied than when Christians continue to live in the past. Forget the past and press forward. Press on, though criticized. Press on, though the way be hard and long. Press on, though enemies oppose. Press on.

Point One

Association with Jesus.

How are we to associate with Jesus? Not by having our own righteousness which is of the law, but the righteousness which is by faith in Jesus Christ (see Philippians 3:9).

Not by having my way, for "my ways are not your ways" says the Lord. His ways are higher, purer, better and altogether holy (see Isaiah 55:8).

If we would have power with God, we must fix our hearts upon Christ and His righteousness. Seek to win Him as the runner wins the prize. Seek to make Him as the sailor makes the port he is bound for. The indication is we will need Him.

The wind is going to blow; the rain will fall; friends will forsake you; the devil will shoot at you. But if you can win Christ you will be safe: "If Christ be for us" (see Romans 8:31).

CONCLUSION

Be found in him as the manslayer was found in the city of refuge where he was safe from the avenger of blood.

Be found in Him for He is a friend in trouble.
Be found in Him for He is a rock in a weary land.
Be found in Him for He will make your enemies your footstool.
Be found in Him for He can make a way where there is no way.
Be found in Him for He will make up your dying bed.

"Father, I stretch my hand to thee,
No other help I know. . ."

How can I sink with such a prop as my eternal God?

SECTION TWO
REV. A. L. WINGFIELD

Reverend A. L. Wingfield, my uncle, has the distinction of pastoring longer than any in the Wingfield family. His pastoral ministry spanned forty years. Born on December 21, 1925 in Franklin County, Virginia, he was educated in the Pittsburgh Public School District, having graduated from Taylor Allderdice High School. He furthered his education by attending the University of Pittsburgh and the Reformed Presbyterian Theological Seminary.

Reverend Wingfield was licensed to preach in 1952 at the Trinity Baptist Church of Pittsburgh under the pastorate of his father, Reverend W. W. Wingfield, Sr. On January 26, 1954, he accepted the call to pastor the First Baptist Church of Finleyville, Pennsylvania. He was the third member of the Wingfield family to pastor this congregation and served there for fourteen years.

In October, 1967, Reverend Wingfield received the call to pastor the Vermont Baptist Church of Creighton, Pennsylvania where he served for twenty-six years. He led this congregation in a complete renovation of the church edifice.

Included among his civic activities were his service as chairperson for the Western District in the state of Pennsylvania for the Lott Carey Baptist Foreign Mission Convention, and a term as area Vice Moderator of the Alle-Kiski area for the Allegheny Union Baptist Association. He was also a member of the Baptist Ministers Conference of Pittsburgh and Vicinity.

After forty years of pastoring, Pastor Wingfield died suddenly on November 14, 1993 in service, having just concluded giving the charge to his seventh son in the ministry.

THE CONTEXT

The ministry of A. L. Wingfield ran concurrently with his father as well as his brother and nephew. His ministry spanned through the economic upheaval of the steel industry in Western Pennsylvania. These times represented a transition in the church, ushered in by a new open-minded spirit of regional and national life. Northern migration from the South had slowed. In fact, the trend had reversed and those in the North returned to the South to escape harsh winters and declining economic conditions in the North. At this time, Black churches began to acknowledge the role of women in ministry. Thus, among his seven sons in the ministry, he also had three daughters.

The context for ministry also revealed the diminishing role of the Black church as the center for communal life. With the emergence of the computer age and the increasing affluence of African-Americans, the church became less important within the life of the Black community. Racism continued its unchecked ascendancy in the 1980s, however, under the presidency of Ronald Reagan and George Bush.

It was into this context that A. L. Wingfield preached. He remained passionate about the church and its role in society, and expressed concern regarding the apathy of people toward the church. He was the resident theologian of the family, yet always focused on practical applications to life situations. Thus, his wisdom was sought by many.

He was also meticulous about the development of sermons. This is evident in the manuscripts that follow. He was essentially a flat-footed preacher. He did not move from behind the pulpit much, though he would at times to help make an illustration.

REAL PREACHING[5]

"The word that God putteth in my mouth, that shall I speak" (Numbers 22:38).

"As ye go, preach" (Matthew 10:7).

INTRODUCTION

I have been surrounded by preachers, both from within and from without our family circle, all of my life. My sainted father before me was a preacher, and, I might add, a preacher par excellence, and a pastor of the first magnitude. His brother (my uncle) before him was a strong and forceful "contender for the faith which was once delivered unto the saints" (Jude 3).

My own brother, who incidentally surrendered his commission some seven years ago, and has joined the ranks of the immortals, was an authoritative voice "crying in the wilderness, prepare ye the way of the Lord." And now his son, Richard Warren Wingfield, has picked up the mantle, and has set sail upon the turbulent, and yet tranquil waters of the gospel ministry.

And I myself have been trying to preach the gospel, to represent my Master for more than three decades. Now, I hasten to point out that I have not nor do I ever expect to reach perfection, nor attain to the heights of many of you, my colleagues in the gospel ministry. The point I am trying to make is simply this: By the grace of God, I have acquired some knowledge on the subject of preaching and preachers, and I come today to share that knowledge with you.

Now, I hasten to point out that I cannot preach with the power and persuasion of the Apostle Paul; I cannot speak with the courage and conviction of Simon Peter; I cannot expound upon the Word with the smooth eloquence of Apollos; in fact, I cannot even match the eloquence of many of you who are seated at my feet this very hour. And yet I feel, based upon the wisdom and knowledge I have acquired across the years, I am qualified to preach from the subject "Real Preaching."

I here recall to mind a statement the late Dr. William Harris, Sr., made many years ago during one of his several lectures on the subject entitled "The Pulpit and the Preacher." He said, "About the worst thing that can be said about a preacher is that he can't preach."

A preacher may not be a scholar; that is to say, he may not be able to read the Greek, or Latin, or the Hebrew. Indeed, he may be somewhat limited insofar as the letter is concerned, but he must be able to preach. He may not rate high as a leader or an organizer—and every preacher, especially pastors, should possess some leadership ability. He may not hold the distinction of being a great and dynamic leader, but he must be able to preach.

He may not excel as an administrator—and every preacher, especially pastors, should possess some administrative ability. Indeed, he may be totally ignorant as to the fine points of business administration, but he must be able to preach.

He may not ever sit in the seat of the mighty, nor converse with the elders and rulers of the land. His name may never appear in the headlines of the morning's paper, but he must be able to preach.

---

[5]This sermon was preached at the installation service of the Rev. Richard Wingfield at the St. Paul Baptist Church of Donora, Pennsylvania on September 17, 1989.

Well, we must answer that question by asking another question, What, or who is a real preacher? We may not relish the idea of dealing with this question, but deal with it we must: for "real preaching" issues forth from "real preachers." And before we can determine what real preaching is we must first determine who or what is a real preacher.

A real preacher is, first and foremost, a representative of the Most High God; a crowned and commissioned ambassador of the Lord Jesus Christ. He is a proclaimer of Christ Jesus, the Holy One of Israel, the Messiah of ancient prophecy, the incarnate Son of the living God. A real preacher reverences God and defends His honor, and considers the Master's business preeminent, more excellent, by far, than all other business. A real preacher does not, I repeat, does not adulterate or corrupt the Word of God. He does not delete from nor add to the Word. He does not interpret the Word falsely (2 Timothy 2:15). He does not speculate or preach secular philosophy or abstract theory:

> "For we preach not ourselves, but Christ Jesus the Lord:
> and ourselves your servants for Jesus's sake" (2 Corinthians 4:5).

> "We don't go around preaching about ourselves, but about Christ
> Jesus as Lord. All we say of ourselves is that we are your-slaves
> because of what Jesus has done for us"
> —The Living Bible.

Negative: Nowadays, if a man is a "preacher," if he has the title "Reverend" in front of his name, many people are somewhat inclined to view him with suspicion. Why? Because so many professing preachers have made a complete mess of preaching. They have developed all kinds of games and gimmicks and employed all kinds of psychological trickery to woo and win support to themselves. They have used charm and charisma, and even their message, to establish kingdoms for themselves.

We are living in an era in which self-styled preachers (I call them spiritual quacks or religious charlatans) have done a great deal of damage to the cause of Christ. There are preachers who are proclaiming false and bizarre teachings, leading countless thousands down the primrose path to degradation and ruin. Moreover, we are living in a time of the personality cult.

Today, the so-called "successful" preachers are those who have made it in terms of their own personalities. There are biographies written about them; and in some cases, they write their own autobiographies. They tell how much they pray, how often they read their Bible, how long they fast, how much they love their wives, and how good they are to their children.

Hear me now: Any preacher who continuously emphasizes himself, who draws attention to himself, and is in the preaching business for monetary benefits, is not a real preacher and is not worthy to be identified with real preachers.

Summation: Who is a real preacher? A real preacher is one who speaks in the authority of the Lord Jesus Christ; who possesses a greater than ordinary knowledge of God; who is endowed with an even greater ability to communicate that knowledge to others and does so without reservation, without compromise, without apology, and, if you please, without expectation of reward.

But then, bear in mind, my brethren, that it is possible for one to possess each of these attributes, and yet not be a real preacher. The principle character here in my text is a classic case in point. If ever a man possessed great knowledge of God; if ever a man possessed great ability to communicate that knowledge, the prophet Balaam was that man. When King Balak sent a delegation to the prophet with a request that he pronounce a curse upon the children of Israel, the prophet replied, and note the eloquence with which he speaks:

> "How shall I curse, whom God hath not cursed?
> Or how shall I defy, whom the Lord hath not defied?
> From the top of the rocks I see him,
> and from the hills I behold him:
> Who can count the dust of Jacob,
> and number the fourth part of Israel?
> Let me die the death of the righteous,
> and let my last days be like his" (Numbers 23:8-10).

Who, then, is a real preacher? A real preacher is one who receives periodic visits from God, who is instructed by the Holy Spirit in the fine arts of preaching, and who follows His instructions to the letter. But once again, we must bear in mind, my brethren, that it is possible for one to be visited by God, to be instructed by him, and yet not be a real preacher.

When the prophet invited the king's delegation to abide with him until he could, once again, consult God in this matter of cursing the children of Israel, God came to him and said, "Thou shalt not go with them; Thou shalt not curse the people: for they are blessed" (Numbers 22:12).

Note carefully: The prophet received his instructions from the Lord, and followed them to the letter, but his heart was not right. He should have sent the delegation back to Balak at once with a firm refusal to comply with the king's request. But his longing for the reward that the king offered led him to keep them overnight and, by doing so, placed his position and his very soul in grave jeopardy.

Well, then, who is a real preacher? A real preacher is one who sees visions of things to come and interprets or explains those visions in the light of contemporary times. But once again, we must bear in mind that the prophet Balaam was a man of vision. He, too, saw visions of the Almighty. In fact, his prophecy concerning the coming Messiah is as clear as any prophecy in the Old Testament:

> "I shall see him, but not now: I shall behold him, but not nigh:
> there shall come a star out of Jacob, and a scepter shall rise out of Israel, and shall
> smite the corners of Moab, and destroy all the children of Seth" (Numbers 24:17).

Point Two
Real Preaching

"The word that God putteth in my mouth, that shall I speak."

I shall never forget the good counsel one of my instructors gave me at the very outset of my ministry: "My son," he said, "God gives every preacher but one sermon, one basic theme, and the preacher spends the remainder of his days developing that one theme. So then, my son, your prayer should be, 'Speak, Lord, for thy servant heareth'" (1 Samuel 3:9).

Hear me now: I do not concern myself with the message or the preaching ability of my colleagues in the ministry. The word that God putteth in my mouth, that shall I speak.

I do not blush, nor look with envy upon a brother or sister who outranks me in the ministry. The word that God putteth in my mouth, that shall I speak.

I do not ridicule or rebuff a preacher, nor seek to undermine his ministry simply because he is more popular with the people than I am. The word that God putteth in my mouth, that shall I speak.

It may not be a long sermon; it may not be a sermon seasoned with long, elaborate phrases and high-sounding platitudes. Indeed, it may consist of only one sentence, seventeen words, and seventy-one letters: The word that the Lord putteth in my mouth, that shall I speak.

The world is hungry—preach the Word! Men need pardon—preach the Word! The world needs principles and power of a new life—preach the Word!

Men and women need hope for the future—preach the Word! Jews need liberty and Gentiles need light—preach the Word! The bereaved and broken-hearted need comfort—preach the Word! The downtrodden needs hope and the sinner needs salvation—preach the Word!

SAVED BY HOPE

"For we are saved by hope" (Romans 8:24).

INTRODUCTION

Hope is something which a certain Bible scholar calls "the real riches." The Apostle Paul refers to it very often in his epistles. He says it (hope) is one of the things that abides.

> Whether there be prophecies, they shall fail; whether there be tongues,
> they shall cease; whether there be knowledge, it shall vanish away. . . .
> And now abideth faith, hope, and charity, these three; but the
> greatest of these is charity (1 Corinthians 13:8, 13).

How long hope will abide, Paul did not say. Whether it will go with us into the beyond seems to be a question open to debate. Love will! Love is clearly eternal. Faith will some day be exchanged for sight. Hope will be lost in glad and glorious fruition. Hence, the remark of another certain Bible scholar,

> Hope is manifestly terrestrial. Its very existence must be lost in the overwhelming realities of futurity. The future can have no room either for fear or its opposite, hope, for fear anticipates suffering and hope, enjoyment. But where both are final, fixed and full, what place remains for either? Fear and hope are of the earth, earthly—the pale and trembling daughters of mortality—for in heaven we can fear no change and in hell no change is to be feared.

It is not alike clear to all persons that faith and hope will not be needed in the other world. It is, I think, clear to all, they (faith and hope) are needed in *this* world. They have been likened to "twin sisters, both beautiful as they can be and very often mistaken the one for the other." Says a well-known writer,

> "Between them, there is this clear difference, that while hope expects, faith inspects; while hope is like Mary, looking upward, faith is like Martha, looking at-ward; while the light on the eyes of hope is high, the light in the eyes of faith is strong; while hope trembles in expectation, faith is quiet in possession.

> "Hope leaps out toward what will be; faith holds on to what is. Hope idealizes, faith realizes. Faith sees, hope foresees. Faith is the substance of things hoped for, the evidence of things not seen; hope is the anchor of the soul, sure and steadfast, entering into that within the veil."

Now, my text says, "We are saved by hope." Ordinarily, we do not think of hope as performing this office. Elsewhere in the Scriptures, we read that we are saved by faith. In another place, it is distinctly stated that we are saved by grace. I am quite sure most of you will recall other passages in the Bible where it is said, "We are saved by Jesus Christ."

It is just such seemingly contradictions as these that the critics like to get hold of. They (critics) make the most of them against the Bible without trying to see if they could not be honestly explained and harmonized.

Without attempting any learned and/or theological exposition of this passage of Scripture, let us agree that it is only doing as we ought to do with any book—to try to catch the meaning of the writer, to interpret his words in their connection.

When Paul says hope saves, he may mean in a different way from faith, or grace, or the Lord Jesus. There are different kinds of salvation. A man may be saved from drowning, from bankruptcy, from violence or despair, without reference to the salvation of his soul from sin and death. It will be fitting for us to inquire if the Apostle had not some special thought of this kind in view when he wrote these words of my text.

If we examine this eighth chapter of Romans, we shall find Paul is dealing with the subject of suffering as a result of sin and by what means we may hope, eventually, to find deliverance. Indirectly, he shows that sin has brought its pain and penalty on all creation.

"We know" he says, "that the whole creation groaneth and travaileth in pain together until now" (Romans 8:22). Even we who have been redeemed from the condemnation of the law and from the curse of sin have not, as yet, been freed from its consequences. We suffer from its effects every day of our lives and we shall so long as we live in this world.

But this is not to be to us an occasion of sadness and despair because a time of entire exemption is coming. We have been adopted into God's redeemed family through the redemption purchased by Jesus, the Christ of God. We are going where sin and suffering cannot come. Even these poor bodies, so full of aches and pains, are to be redeemed. This is our hope, and in this hope we wait with patience, confidence, and uncomplaining:

> "For we are saved by hope; but hope that is seen is not hope;
> for what a man seeth, why doth he yet hope for? But if we
> hope for what we see not, then do we with patience wait for it" (Romans 8:24)

It is with a desire to illustrate and enforce this truth of the text, for your comfort and encouragement, that I ask you to consider two or three things further about this hope which, in order to distinguish it, I will call Christian hope. The first thing which I wish to say about Christian hope is that it is:

Point One
A safe hope

Hope is a part and power of human nature. But all hope is not Christian and is not safe or sure. All men have hope, but not good hopes. The Bible says bad men have hopes, some of which can never be realized: "The hope of the hypocrite shall be cut off" (Job 27:8), and "The hope of the unjust man perisheth" (Proverbs 11:7).

How many men have hopes that are built on an insecure or false foundation! Life is full of blighted hopes and yet, the only thing that makes life tolerable to thousands of persons is their hope. Some are hoping, as it were, against hope. They have been disappointed times without number. Yet, somehow they can hope again. And when hope gives out, all is gone. Then comes collapse, mental disorder, madness, suicide. Oh, how many such instances there are—blasted hopes and ruined lives!

Human hopes are treacherous. They are so often ill-formed and poorly founded. They are like the house that was built on the sand. When the wind and the floods came and beat upon them they fall and, oftentimes, great is the fall of them—great in its calamity and consequences. Such, too often, is the case with hopes built on human promises—on the gains, pleasures, friendships, fortunes of this world.

Christian hope is a safe hope because it builds on the promises of God which, incidentally, cannot be broken. Whatever God has promised for this life—pardon, peace, prosperity—if the conditions of the promise are met, hope is never disappointed.

Experiencing so much of God's goodness here, surely we can trust him for whatever is promised hereafter. So the psalmist says: "Happy is he whose hope is in the Lord his God" (Psalm 146:5). And the prophet, Jeremiah, echoes the same thought when he says, "Blessed is the man whose hope the Lord is" (Jeremiah 17:7).

These testimonies could be supported from the experience of thousands of God's children showing that there are no blighted and blasted hopes when they are built on the sure promises of God's Word.

Christian hope is a safe hope because it has a moral basis. There is nothing in it which disappoints or demoralizes. Its uplift is heavenly. Any society of men who would live, in the moral sense of life, must be looking forward to something. Precious must be the inheritance of the past to every true-hearted and generous man. What is the past without the future? What is a memory unaccompanied by hope? In the case of the individual, as in the case of the nation and Church, high and earnest purpose will die outright if it is permitted to sink into the place of perpetual retrospect. Another thing which may be said about Christian hope is that it is:

Point Two

A sustaining hope

Who of us does not need such a hope? We need it in our work. Most of us are willing to labor, and some of us labor too hard, if only we can see the return or reward of our labor.

In Christian work, it is peculiarly true that we have to sow in hope and till in hope. Very often the sower and the tiller never see the harvest. "One soweth and another reapeth" (John 4:37). This is not always so. There is another Scripture which says, "They that sow in tears shall reap in joy. He that goeth forth and weepeth, bearing precious seed, shall doubtless come again with rejoicing, bringing his sheaves with him" (Psalm 126:5-6).

The harvest is, however, often delayed for one reason or another, and we have to work and wait. Now, hope helps us. It keeps us from becoming impatient and disheartened. The Scripture says; "It is good that a man should both hope and quietly wait for the salvation of the Lord" (Lamentations 3:26). Some things cannot be done in a hurry. God's work is important work—work that lasts through all eternity. It takes time to do it and do it well. Some of us want to see, at once, the fruit of our labor and some act as though they expect fruit without much labor.

It is hard to work on and wait—wait and work when energies have grown tired, when resources have given out, when confidence in ourselves and of others is almost exhausted. Hope is the last thing to surrender. It hangs on. It continues to expect. It grips the thing once more and that last grip conquers. We come now, in conclusion, to one other point. A hope that is safe and does so much to sustain must be.

Point Three
A saving hope

This is Paul's claim. If any man had reason to lose confidence in men and in the world in general, Paul was the man. The reason he was so hopeful for the Gospel, the church, the future, and for himself, was because he had confidence in all that Jesus said and did.

To him these things were real, the abiding, the most blessed things for time and eternity. So he could speak of hope as an anchor to the soul, sure and steadfast. With all his perplexities, stripes, shipwrecks, imprisonments, he is the most cheery and courageous soul of that or almost any other period.

What helped and sustained Paul? It was this hope. "I reckon," he said, "the sufferings of this present time are not worthy to be compared with the glory which shall be revealed in us" (Romans 8:18). "If in this life only," he said, "we have hope in Christ, we are of all men most miserable" (1 Corinthians 15:19).

Thank God for a hope that will not fail us at the end. This world is full of false hopes, of broken dreams, of heartaches, and disappointments. Life does not bring to one-half the people what they thought it would bring. Even those who have been sated with the good things of this world find them losing their relish as life wears on. What is all the good of this world, when attained, if the soul of man comes to the end of life empty and poor, without hope, a good hope of heaven and without God.

As Sir Walter Scott lay dying, he said to his son-in-law,

> "I may have but a minute to speak to you.
> My dear, be a good man—be virtuous—be
> religious—be a good man. Nothing else will give
> you any comfort when you come to lie here."

You have heard the story of a great king who sent his servants to level a forest; to plow it and plant it, and bring back to him a harvest. One laborer was named faith, another industry, another patience, another self-denial, another importunity.

To cheer their toil, they took along their sister, Hope. While they worked she (Hope) sang. When they became discouraged, she found a way to cheer them. When they saw nothing but stumps and soil, she talked about the harvest.

So they kept at it, until finally they shouted harvest-home, because Hope never refrained from singing and encouraging.

God has placed us here to cultivate His vineyard, and return to Him the harvest. When things look dark and discouraging to us, let us hear this song of hope, breaking on our ears with heavenly sweetness. And let us realize that we are sustained and comforted and saved by hope.

My hope is built on nothing less,

Than Jesus's blood and righteousness;
I dare not trust the sweetest frame,
But wholly lean on Jesus's name.

"When darkness veils his lovely face,
I rest on his unchanging grace;
In every high and stormy gale,
My anchor holds within the veil.

"His oath, His covenant and blood,
Support me in the whelming flood;
When all around my soul gives way,
He then is all my hope and stay.

On Christ, the solid Rock, I stand,
All other ground is sinking sand.

KEEP LOOKING FOR THE LIGHT

"Now when Jesus was born in Bethlehem of Judea in the days of Herod the king, behold, there came wise men from the east to Jerusalem, saying, 'Where is he that is born King of the Jews? For we have seen his star in the east and are come to worship him. . . .When they saw the star, they rejoiced with exceeding great joy"
(Matthew 2:1-2,10).

INTRODUCTION

It is a matter of considerable controversy as to the distance that the wise men traveled in order to pay homage to the Christ child. Some Bible scholars contend that they came all the way from the Tigris and Euphrates Valley in Mesopotamia, while other scholars maintain that they came from as far away as Damascus, which was, and yet is, a part of the land of Arabia.

There is, however, one mailer that all of the scholars seem to agree upon; that is, the Wise Men, after having seen this strange phenomenon in the eastern skies, went forth in search of *that star up yonder* and were in transit almost two years before finally reaching their destination, Bethlehem.

And when we consider the mode and means of travel in those days, it does not require much imagination to visualize the dangers, the difficulties, the hardships, the frustrating moments they must have experienced before finally reaching journey's end.

But having seen the "star in the East," and recognizing the fact that this was no ordinary star, they were determined not to succumb to despair, not to abandon hope, until their hopes and dreams had become reality.

They hymnolgist, William Cowper, in his now famous hymn, "God Moves in a Mysterious Way," declared,

> "God moves in a mysterious way
> His wonders to perform;
> He plants his footstep on the sea,
> And rides on every storm."

Now, the mysterious workings of the Almighty are, once again, made manifest in the coming of the wise men to Bethlehem. The wise men were Gentiles, not Jews; heathens, and not of the chosen people of God. They were not versed in the Scriptures; they had never read the prophecies of Isaiah, or Amos, or Joel, which foretold of the coming of the Messiah. And yet they were the ones who alerted the Jewish community that the ancient prophecy had finally been fulfilled, and that the Messiah had indeed made his entry into the world.

Though heathens, having no background in the Jewish system of government, or their culture, or their heritage, after having seen the star, gave themselves no rest until that star "came and stood over where they young child was" (Matthew 2:9).

Though "aliens from the commonwealth of Israel, and strangers from the covenants of promise," they kept looking for the light. Though frustrated by Herod on every hand, and, doubtless, oftentimes sidetracked in their search for the star of Bethlehem, they never once wavered; they kept looking for the light.

For they believed, based upon what they had heard, or what had been revealed to them, that the Babe of Bethlehem came to bear the sins of the world, to be the Savior of the world. To be not only "the glory of God's people Israel," but also "a light to lighten the Gentiles."

And, so, though kings in their own right, though themselves men of pomp and circumstance, they recognized the fact that they were walking in spiritual darkness and were in desperate need of the Light of Life.

Point One
The inspriation of Christmas

You and I, like the wise men of old, may be far from home. You and I may be caught on the horns of a dilemma and know not which way to go. You and I may be gripped in the tight fist of circumstances, or caught up in the beastly jaws of adversity. But if we do not despair of hope, if we keep looking for the light, the star of hope will, one day, come into full focus. And if we follow that star, it will lead us to peace and joy and happiness in the Lord Jesus Christ.

A. And I hasten to point out, and most emphatically so, that these are precious commodities. They cannot be purchased with gold, silver, or precious stones. They come as the direct result of having a personal encounter with the Babe of Bethlehem, who has become the King of kings and Lord of lords. That's why we sing,

> Joy to the world, the Lord is come;
> Let earth receive her King!
> Let every heart prepare him room,
> And heaven and nature sing.

B. For some people, the Christmas story is only a sentimental tale about a little baby, born in a stable, or it's a festive occasion when we spend a lot of money buying gifts. But Christmas means more than that. If I may quote the gospel writer, John:

"In the beginning was the Word and the Word was with God, and the Word was God. . . .
And the Word was made flesh and dwelt among us; and we beheld his
glory, the glory as of the only begotten of the Father, full of grace and truth" (John 1:1, 14).

Point Two
There's got to be a morning after.

No matter how dark and benighted the way may become, there's got to be a morning after. No matter how tiresome and tedious the journey, there's got to be a morning after. No matter how many obstacles are placed in the way, there's got to be a morning after. "Trials dark on every hand

and we cannot understand," but, there's got to be a morning after.

A. [To you, a] Laid off steel worker; benefits running out, bills piling up, no meal in the barrel, no oil in the cruse, don't self-destruct, don't take your own life, there's got to be a morning after.

B. [You] Senior citizens struggling to make ends meet, cast down in spirit and soul, there's got to be a morning after.

C. Oh, wife, oh husband; marriage ripping apart at the seams, your castle in the air is crumbling to the ground, there's got to be a morning after.

Cruel winds of adversity may blow, but keep looking for the light. Hardships may dot your pathway, but keep looking for the light. Dreams and aspirations may be frustrated, but that's all right, just keep looking for the light.

Point Three
The Light: Jesus Christ

"There was a man sent from God, whose name was John. He was not that light, but was sent to bear witness of that Light. That was the true light, which lighteth every man that cometh into this world" (John 1:6-9).

"Then spake Jesus again unto them, saying, "I am the light of the world; he that followeth me shall not walk in darkness, but shall have the light of life" (John 8:12).

I know an old deacon (and thank God for good deacons) in a certain Baptist church, always going around singing,

"Hark! the herald angels sing,
Jesus, the Light of the world;
Glory to the newborn King,
Jesus, the Light of the world."

"We'll walk in the light, beautiful light,
Come where the dewdrops of mercy are bright;
Shine all around us by day and by night,
Jesus, the Light of the world."

Don't let your dreams die! Don't let your star of hope fade out of sight! Keep looking for the light. The wise men did not wait for the "Light" to find them; they went in search of the Light. Keep looking for the light!

ATHEISM AND THE BIBLE

"The fool hath said in his heart, 'There is no God'" (Psalm 53:1).

"Only a fool would say to himself, 'There is no God'.
And why does he say it? Because of his wicked heart,
his dark and evil deeds. His life is corroded with sin" (The Living Bible).

INTRODUCTION

The shadows of atheism and agnosticism are deepening. Atheism today dares to raise its voice in defiance of God and His Christ, not only in faraway lands, but in America. From persecution they (the Pilgrim fathers) fled, to worship God as they pleased, they came. The Bible was their chart and compass. No thought had they of infidelity. That remained for their children, children wise in their own conceits: "The fool hath said in his heart, 'There is no God." They did not wish to be classified as "fools."

Voltaire, Ingersoll, and Paine are no more. They are but individual advocates of atheism. Voltaire spent his life trying to prove that there is no God. He once said that within a hundred years there would not be a Bible in existence. Well, the atheist is gone and, as if to remind the world of his folly, his own house for a time became the headquarters of the British and Foreign Bible Society.

Point One

Worn-out arguments

As to the arguments of the present-day atheists and their attacks on the Bible and its Author—they are but the old worn out statements of the infidels of a generation ago. Every argument has been answered again and again. Not one will hold water. In spite of all that has been written, it yet remains for someone to prove that there is no God; to prove that the Bible is unreliable and fallible, to prove that men are not sinners needing a Savior, to prove that there is no heaven and no hell.

No infidel, no atheist has ever yet produced such proof. They have ridiculed and mocked, they have argued and questioned, but they have never proved. They cannot and they know it. A certain infidel once said, "I would gladly give $150,000 to have proved to my satisfaction that these is no such place as hell." Poor man! He might have offered a hundred million dollars with as little hope of success.

The Bible has been with us for centuries. It claims to be the Word of God. Men have believed in heaven and hell for generations. It remains now for the atheists to prove the contrary. And while they have been hammering away at the Word of God, the Bible has marched right on. Infidels and agnostics have gone to their doom, but the Bible is still here: "The grass withereth, the flower fadeth; but the Word of our God shall stand forever" (Isaiah 40:8), and "Heaven and earth shall pass away, but my Word shall not pass away" (Matthew 24:35).

Point Two

Cause and effect

To a person of average intelligence, the argument of cause and effect in itself, it seems to me, is unanswerable. For instance, I pick up a watch and examine its works and know, at once, that it did not fall from the skies, neither did it grow by the roadside. Ordinary reason tells me that it had a maker, that someone designed it, that only an intelligent being could have invented it.

I see an automobile. I have never known one to be born. It didn't just happen. A glance tells me that it was built for a special purpose and, immediately, I think of a first cause and conclude that it must have been fashioned by an intelligent being.

I look at a house and I know that it had a builder. An effect always presupposes a cause. Robinson Crusoe finds the print of a man's foot on the sand. He does not waste time trying to invent some new theory. He comes immediately to the irrefutable conclusion that it was made by a man and that a man must have been on the island.

I see planets, sun, moon and stars, and all moving in perfect order, each in its own prescribed orbit. They never clash and they are right on time. I see plants, trees, flowers, animals, birds, fish, men and instinctively, I look for a Creator, a designer, a mastermind. Some all-powerful, intelligent being I know must have designed and created all of them. Hence, there simply must be a God somewhere.

Why does the atheist not want God? He wants a watchmaker for a watch. He wants an automobile manufacturer for a car. He wants an architect and builder for a house. Why not a Creator for a universe? There can be one answer. He is not right with God and, consequently, does not want to meet Him.

Point Three

Who wrote the Bible?

In answer to the eternal question regarding the origin of the Bible, I submit that it was written by one of five different companies of men—good men, bad men, deceived men, men under Satanic influence, or men under the power of the Holy Spirit. Outside of these five companies, there are no others.

A. Did good men write the Bible?

No, they did not, as it claims to come from God. If good men had written it and then tried to pass it off as a message from heaven, they would cease to be good men—they would be deceivers. Good men would not claim to be inspired if they were not inspired; neither could they say, "Thus saith the Lord," if the Lord had not spoken. Whereas if the Lord had spoken through them, it would cease to be their production. Hence, good men did not write this book.

B. Could bad men have written it?

No, it would be an utter impossibility for bad men to produce such a masterpiece. Can you imagine wicked men writing the epistle to the Ephesians or to the Hebrews? The glorious truths here unfolded are as far above their conception as heaven is above the earth.

Moreover, bad men would not pronounce their own doom and write a book that would consign them to eternal punishment. The Bible is a book that speaks of matchless grace; but it also speaks of death, hell, fire, and judgment, so we could not expect wicked men to produce such a book as the Bible.

C. Did deceived men write the Bible?

Many would tell us that the writers were sincere, simple, and honest men, but they were deceived by Jewish superstition. That from a heap of historical and mythical writings they gathered together sixty-six books and, in their ignorance, gave to them divine honors.

Well, what about the prophetic utterances of these men, now fulfilled in history? Do deceived men write real prophecy and correct history? I think not! Deceived men did not give us the prophecies of Daniel, Ezekiel, Jeremiah, Amos, Obadiah, Jonah, and the likes. No, no, deceived men did not write the Scriptures, as those who are deceived do not write truth, and the Scriptures are true.

D. Was it Satanic influence?

The fourth company of men on our list is a company under Satanic influence. Could such a company have written the Bible? Again we have to reply in the negative. This class may be dismissed at once as the Bible reveals the fall, history, character, and doom of Satan. And he, Satan, would certainly not lead and inspire men to write such an exposure.

Moreover, Satan is spoken of throughout the Bible as a liar, deceiver, accuser, murderer, and the like. His awful doom, without hope, is revealed in the Scriptures, as well as the doom of the impenitent. These things Satan would seek to hide from the eyes of men. Hence, it necessarily follows, that such a company could not have written the Bible.

E. Was it written by the Holy Spirit?

We have only one class now remaining who could possibly have written this book; namely, men inspired, yes, and energized by the Holy Spirit.

> "For we have not been telling you fairy tells when we explained
> to you the power of our Lord Jesus Christ and his coming again.

> "My own eyes have seen his splendor and his glory; I was there
> on the holy mountain when he shone out with honor given him
> by God, his Father; I heard that glorious, majestic voice calling
> down from heaven, saying, 'This is my much-loved Son; I am
> well pleased with him'.

> "So we have seen and proved that what the prophets said came
> true. You will do well to pay close attention to everything they
> have written, for, like lights shining into dark corners, their words
> help us to understand many things that otherwise would be dark
> and difficult.

> "But when you consider the wonderful truth of the prophet's words

then the light will dawn on your souls and Christ, the morning star,
will shine in your hearts.

"For no prophecy recorded in Scripture was ever thought up by the
prophet himself It was the Holy Spirit within these godly men who
gave them the true message from God" (2 Peter 1:16-21, The Living Bible).

Yes, the Bible was written by men divinely inspired and is a perfect treasure of heavenly instruction. It has God for its Author, salvation for its end, and truth without any mixture of error for its subject matter. It contains the principles by which God shall judge the world, and is the supreme standard by which all human conduct, creeds, and opinions shall be tried.

Point Four

A day of reckoning

A day of reckoning is coming. A hundred years from now you will be somewhere. Death does not end all. And what the atheist and the agnostic fear most is death and its consequences. The atheist only thinks he is an atheist. Deep down in his heart he knows that there is a God somewhere.

In the silent hours of the night, he fears the God he opposes and dreads, above everything else, the thought of that day when he will meet Him face to face:

"It is a fearful thing to fall into the hands of the living God" (Hebrews 10:31).

"It is appointed unto men once to die, but after this the judgment" (Hebrews 9:27).

You cannot get away from it. God will see to it that you keep His appointment. Death, first, then judgment.

Point Five

Deathbed witnesses

Now, in closing, let me quote the last words of just a few skeptics and unbelievers. Hear what they have to say on their deathbeds; these men and women who dare to attack God and His Word.

Thomas Paine: He cried out in a sudden burst of emotion, even distressful emotion,

"O Lord, help me! God, help me! Jesus Christ, help me"! Repeating the same expression without the least variations in a tone that alarmed the house wherein he died.

Voltaire: In one of his visits, his doctor found him in the greatest agonies, exclaiming with utmost honor, "I am abandoned by God and man." Then he said, "Doctor, I will give you half of what I am worth if you will give me six months' life." The doctor answered, "Sir, you cannot live six weeks." Voltaire replied, "Then I shall go to hell," and soon after, died.

Frances Newport: "Oh, the insufferable pangs of hell and damnation!" and then expired.

Gibbon: "All is dark and dreadful." Asking his wife for a glass of water, he said, "I will not be able to get anywhere I am going." He drank it greedily, then looking his wife in the face, exclaimed, "Oh, Martha, Martha, you have sealed my everlasting damnation!" and died.

Jennie Gordon: "The fiends, they come; Oh save me! They drag me down! Lost, lost, lost." A moment later, she said, "Bind me, ye chains of darkness," and died.

Thomas Scott: "Until this moment, I thought there was neither a God nor a hell. Now, I know and feel that there are both, and I am doomed to perdition by the just judgment of the Almighty."

Point Six

Deathbed scenes of believers

John Payson's death: "I know I am dying, but my deathbed is a bed of roses; I have no thorns planted on my dying pillow. Heaven already is begun. I die a safe, easy, happy death."

John Wesley's death: "Best of all, God is with us." As they wet his lips, he said, "We thank thee, oh Lord, for all thy mercies."

Martin Luther's death: "Father, into thy hands I commit my spirit, for Thou hast redeemed me, Thou God of truth."

Catherine Booth's homegoing: "The waters are rising, but so am I. I am not going under, but over." Her last words were, "Till the day breaks and the shadows flee away."

John Bunyan: "We shall meet e'er long, to sing the new song, and remain happy forever in a world without end. Take me, Jesus, for I come to Thee."

The Apostle Paul: "I am ready to be offered up and the time of my departure is at hand."

Tell me, atheist; tell me, agnostic; tell me, infidel; tell me, skeptic; tell me, unbeliever; tell me, sinner man, when death comes, where are you going to run to?

"It is appointed unto men once to die" (Hebrews 9:27). Who said so? God! God said so! The God you despise. The God you reject. What thoughts will be yours in that awful last hour? Will it be death of an atheist or the home-going of a believer?

It is for you to decide. I beseech you, in the name of the Lord Jesus, turn from your atheism and receive the Lord Jesus Christ as your personal Savior.

Do not procrastinate! Do not postpone it! Do not wait until a more opportune time! Do it now! Tomorrow may be too late.

"Right now; right now!
Let the Savior bless your soul
Right now!
Don't put off until tomorrow
What you can do today;
Let the Savior bless you soul
Right now!"

THE GLORY OF THE EASTER SUN

"And, behold, two of them went that same day to a village called Emmaus, which was from Jerusalem about three-score furlongs" (Luke 24:13-35).

INTRODUCTION

Easter morning had come and the Prince of Life has arisen from the dead. But the genuine Easter joy only gradually found its way into the hearts of the disciples and of all those who loved the Lord Jesus. The three women—Mary Magdalene, Mary, the mother of James, and Salome—had stood at the empty tomb of Jesus and had heard the message of the angel: "Ye seek Jesus of Nazareth, which was crucified. He is risen; He is not here; behold the place where they laid him" (Mark 16:6). And yet they fled from the grave and they trembled and were amazed; neither said they anything to any man, for they were afraid.

The two disciples in our gospel lesson are, on the afternoon of this day, going from Jerusalem to Emmaus. They have heard the Easter message but the Easter blessing has not yet entered their hearts. They are telling each other how certain women had frightened them by their words and are sorrowfully wending their way without hope. Yet on the evening of the same Sabbath, the other disciples, excluding Thomas, were assembled behind locked doors "for fear of the Jews." Easter had come, and the glory of the Easter sun had risen over them, but the Easter joy had not yet entered their hearts.. Only when Jesus suddenly entered, and greeting them with his salutation of "Peace be unto you," are we told that the disciples were glad because they saw the Lord.

Please note: The mighty and glorious Easter miracle will be of no benefit to us, dearly beloved, if the Easter sun does not arise in our hearts also; if we do not in faith receive the Easter message; if we do not within ourselves experience the joy and blessing of the Eastertide.

The Lord Jesus is near; He is risen indeed! This is the glorious and blessed message that has been preached for centuries, and that is being preached this day again. You can hear one Easter sermon after another and live through one Easter season after the other, yet this alone will not secure you the joys and the blessings of this sacred memorial day.

Notwithstanding all this, you are today perhaps sorrowful and downcast, lonesome and lonely, as were those women and the two disciples mentioned in the text, or as were the eleven on that first Easter evening. Yet, the rays of the glorious Easter sun must first penetrate your heart and soul, must warm and illumine them, before you can joyfully join in the chorus of praise and thanksgiving, saying, "The Lord is risen indeed, hallelujah."

And to enable you to do this, the text for today is helpful. It is one of the most precious gospel lessons in the whole cycle of the church year. It exhibits to us the joyfulness and friendliness of the risen Lord, and gives us courage to approach Him and seek His communion. It also shows to us in the experience of the two disciples how the Easter sun can arise in our hearts.

It does not often happen that this takes place suddenly, and that it at once appears in all its glory in the poor sinner's heart, as was the case with Saul on his way to Damascus. As is the case with the sun of the solar system, the Easter sun has its dawn and its first rays—the full glory of its light and warmth. We accordingly ask ourselves the question: When does the glory of the Easter sun arise in our hearts? Answer:

I. When Jesus is our constant companion.
II. When Jesus is our faithful teacher.
III. When Jesus is our dearest friend.
IV. When Jesus is our welcome guest.

Let's look at each one of these points as they pertain to the Easter sun arising in our hearts.

Point One

When Jesus is our constant companion.

The two disciples in the text, Cleopas and his companion, are together journeying from Jerusalem to Emmaus. They are filled with the warmest sympathy for each other and know each other. They are speaking to each other of the things that have, in recent days, happened in Jerusalem and yet, their hearts are filled with sorrow, so that the Master, when he comes to them, asks them for the reasons of their sorrow.

Something is the matter with them. Possibly they do not themselves know what the real cause is. They possibly do not understand themselves, and yet their hearts are bowed down, and this is quite apparent in all their conversation. The one cannot relieve the other and the second cannot comfort the first. They stand in need of a companion who understands how to comfort them and to open up for them the fountain of true joy. This Jesus knows, and therefore, He comes to them with the wonderful love and affection and becomes their charming and dear companion.

Our path in life is much like that of the two disciples on their way to Emmaus. It matters not whether it is long or short, if thirty or forty, or fifty, or sixty furlongs. The matter of importance is the company and association we have in this pilgrimage.

That indeed is a pitiable and lamentable soul who must go the way alone without an associate. But even if that soul has many treasures of gold and silver, even if it is full of earthly honors and pleasures, it is nevertheless a soul to be pitied. The longer the way happens to be, the more dreary and forsaken it will be. Again, that soul is to be pitied which makes this way in bad company.

In such company are heard only impure and unclean words, unjust and unholy conversation. But even that soul, too, is to be pitied who goes through life in better company, but still has not the best friend and companion as his associate. Even if a man has a faithful wife and darling children, has friends and relatives with warm hearts, faithful and good in evil days, yet such a soul is poor unless he has also that friend who is the best and most faithful companion on life's journey.

There is a longing and anxiety found in every honest heart and mind that is satisfied by no joy of this world and by no human companionship. This is the longing for truth amid all errors and falsehoods of this world. The longing for the gleams of the glorious sun of truth dispelling the darkness. It is the longing for happiness that will remove the burdens and sorrows of life. It is the longing for the truly good that no power on earth can take away from us. It is the longing for salvation with a firm and unshaken foundation. A longing for peace which "passeth all understanding" (see Philippians 4:7). A longing for life beyond the grave. A longing for the Kingdom that abides to all eternity.

All this Jesus knows! He knows how to cope with the cares, the frustrations, the anxieties, the aggravations, the perplexing problems of life. He knows how to handle the burdens and sorrows we sustain. He knows how to bring joy out of sorrow, peace out of confusion. He knows how to calm the raging sea and reverse the course of nature.

> "Jesus knows all about our struggles,
> He will guide till the day is done;
> There's not a friend like the lowly Jesus,
> No not one! No, not one!"

Point Two

When Jesus is our faithful teacher.

But this is not all: Christ is more than a companion to us. He is also our faithful teacher. Christ does not walk in silence by the side of the two disciples. He inquires of them as to the subject concerning which they were so anxiously conversing. Cleopas thereupon tells Him of their sadness and laments over their disappointed hopes, confesses the doubt and dismay in his own heart, his anxiety between faith and uncertainty, between terror and wonder.

Then the Master first rebukes them for their "foolishness and slowness of heart" and because they have not believed the words which the prophets spoke. Then He becomes Himself their teacher in the gospel and clearly interprets to them the truth that such suffering on the part of the Messiah was in accordance with prediction and the will of God.

What grand interpretation of the Scripture this must have been which the two disciples were privileged to listen to! Therefore, their hearts burned within them as they listened to the words of the wise Teacher of God's Word.

A. Jesus must also be our teacher if the Easter sun is to cast its glorious warmth into our hearts, if the Easter blessing and the Easter joy is to be ours.

1. There are indeed many who recognize Christ as a "prophet mighty in word and deed," who believe that He was a great man and a wise teacher and who honor Him as such. But they do not read the real meaning of His words, nor do they heed His teachings. Therefore, they go their way in darkness and sadness. One joy after the other disappoints them; one hope after the other proves a fleeting shadow. Their hearts waver between doubt and faith, between fear and hope, and therefore they never find real peace and real joy.

2. There are many disciples of the Lord who are walking on such paths and passing through such hours. This friend or that friend has been taken from him; this or that hope has disappointed him. Sadly, he proceeds on his journey. Then He comes who is the true Teacher, Jesus the Lord, interprets the Scriptures, breaks the Bread of Life, opens the fountain, imparts wisdom, knowledge, and understanding.

This is the gospel that was already proclaimed in Paradise. This is the song of jubilee that is reechoed in the golden streets of the Jerusalem that is above. This proclamation and this message of grace must be believed in the heart.

If you permit the Savior to instruct you in this great truth, if you believe the words which He speaks, you are on the right way. The morning dawn of Easter day will be reflected also in your eyes, and the first dewdrops of the blessing of Easter will fall into your heart.

In this light, you will understand the humility and the glory of the Lord Jesus, His work and His life. In this light, you will understand your own life, your own joys, your own sufferings. In this way, you have found the way and the truth; you have learned from that prince of teachers, even Christ Jesus, the risen Lord.

Point Three

When Jesus is our dearest friend.

But this is not all; Christ is more than a companion to us; He is more than a teacher; He must also be your dearest Friend. The hearts of the two disciples begin to burn as they listen to this wonderful stranger. They feel that He is a man who can help them. Their sadness is removed; their hopes are revived; their doubts are gone; their faith is strengthened; their hearts are comforted.

They love this remarkable man more and more. The journey is only too soon at an end. The time has passed all too quickly as the period for parting companionship is at hand. Jesus "made as though he would have gone further." They ask Him to abide with them, as it is toward evening, and the day is far spent.

They cannot persuade themselves to leave the man with whom they have spent such a profitable evening to continue His journey in the night alone. They offer Him the hospitality of their home. They do not want to spend the night without having seen and heard more of this strange associate. They need Him; they are hungry for His words, and for His comfort. Therefore, they ask Him, saying, "Abide with us: for it is toward evening, and the day is far spent."

A. It is not enough, my brother or my sister, that you seek Jesus and are anxious for Him. It does not suffice that you hear His word and believe it with all your heart. Jesus Christ must be the dearest friend of your heart.

1. Your heart must burn for Him. Your daily prayer and petition should be:

> "Abide with me! Fast falls the even tide;
> The darkness deepens—Lord, with me abide!
> When other helpers fail, and comforts flee,
> Help of the helpless, O abide with me!"

B. And Jesus may sometimes seem as though He would pass on, as though He would forsake you. This is at times His method.

Then pray again, "Abide with me," and you will feel the blessing of this prayer. When your sins trouble you, when weighed down by sorrow and the cross, when the evening of your life is approaching, then is He the sweetest and dearest friend of your soul.

Point Four

When Jesus is our welcome guest.

Finally, the risen Christ is also to be your welcome household guest. He does not suffer His friends to ask long; He gladly stays. In fact, He has already decided to stay, and He only feigns as though He would proceed in His journey, because He wants to be asked to remain.

A. He enters the house with them; He seats Himself at the table; He takes bread, blesses it, breaks it, and gives it to them. The disciples, with ever-increasing wonder, watch Him. Then their eyes have been opened and they know the Lord, their beloved Master, even Jesus, the Christ. They recognize Him who has been crucified and has arisen from the dead. It has become Easter and the Easter sun has arisen in their hearts.

B. And this, dearly beloved, is the best of all. Jesus must enter our homes and houses. He must sit down to the table with us. Jesus must be the Lord and Master over our households. We ourselves must ask Him to become such.

Blessed is the house in which the Easter Prince is the real master and housefather. Blessed is the house in which father and mother, parents and children, sit at His feet. Blessed is the house where Jesus, and Jesus only, breaks the bread; where the daily bread is received at His hands, and where He blesses it; where the bread of life is sought at His door, and is asked of Him.

1. In such a house there is the bright light of day; in such a house the glory of the Easter sun spreads happiness and bliss. Here Easter joy and Easter blessing abound.

Blessed be our God for the victory of death given us through the Prince of Peace; for the conquest of hell through our Lord Jesus Christ, who broke the bounds of the tomb, obtained the victory over death, chained Satan to the chariot wheel, liberated the captive, and set the prisoner free.

Blessed be God, who gave us the Easter joy in His beloved, and the rays from whose glorious Easter sun bring cheer and eternal joy to mankind and to every believing Christian. Amen! Amen! Amen!

"I know that me Redeemer lives;
He lives, who once was dead;
To me in grief He comfort gives;
With peace He crowns my head.

He lives, triumphant o'er the grave,
At God's right hand on high,
My ransomed soul to keep and save,
To bless and glorify.

He lives, that I may also live,
And now His grace proclaim;
He lives, that I may honor give
To His most holy name."

CASTING ASIDE HIS GARMENT

"And he, casting away his garment, rose, and came to Jesus" (Mark 10:50).

INTRODUCTION

Blind Bartimaeus sat by the roadside begging. There was no welfare program he could count on. There were no food stamps to supplement his income. There was no association for the blind to which he could turn for help. He was totally at the mercy of those who passed by.

What a tragic situation for any man or woman to be in—sitting by the side of the road begging for someone to notice and to help.

Have you ever been there? Have you ever sat by the roadside begging? Sure you have! If you have ever been young and unsure of yourself, you have sat by the roadside begging.

In my mind's eye, I see a young lady sitting alone on the side of the dance floor. She tries to act like it doesn't matter, but the truth of the matter is that she would give anything if some young fellow would look her way and ask her for a dance.

"Silly" you say. Have you forgotten what it is to be young?

Or, walk through the ward of a hospital or nursing home and see the hands reaching out. They are not reaching out for money or food. They are not destitute; they are not hungry; they only want to know that somebody notices and cares.

Have you ever sat by the side of the road and cried, "Jesus, thou Son of David, have mercy on me"? You have if you have ever sat in an emergency room of a hospital while doctors and nurses administer critical aid to a loved one, or sat beside an open grave as they lowered a loved one into the ground.

You've been there if you have laid awake at night trying to figure out how you were going to feed your family, or pay the mortgage, or how to keep a certain utility company from terminating your service, or how to keep your marriage together, or how to help your child through a difficult period.

The truth of the mailer is that, at some period in our lives, each of us is a blind Bartimeaus, sitting by the side of the road, praying that someone will notice and care.

Point One

The good news for the day, the good news for this very moment, is that Jesus notices and cares.

He noticed blind Bartimaeus. Jesus and His disciples were on the road leading out of Jericho. Their journey took them right by the place where Bartimaeus sat begging alms. When Jesus came near, Bartimaeus cried out, "Jesus, thou son of David, have mercy on me."

Persons round about him tried to get Bartimaeus to be quiet. But he cried out the louder,

"Thou son of David, have mercy on me" (Mark 10:47).

Jesus was moved by this simple plea. He called for Bartimaeus. When he realized that Jesus was calling to him, he leaped to his feet, cast aside his garment, and started toward Jesus.

A. The garment that he cast aside was probably a blanket or loose piece of cloth that beggars in that part of the world carried to protect them from the inclement weather. He didn't want anything to hinder him from coming into the Master's presence, and so, "He, casting aside his garment, rose, and came to Jesus" (Mark 10:50).

B. Oh, but that you and I were that eager to come to Jesus! There is a story that comes out of the days of slavery in this country. The year was 1773. A great revival of religious enthusiasm was sweeping across America. Horseback evangelists were proclaiming the good news of Jesus Christ with great vigor.

They were getting a startling response. Heart were being touched. Lives were being changed. Both whites and blacks heard these traveling preachers gladly. Men and women of both races were converted.

A few months after one of these revivals, a white man and a black man were discussing the effects on their lives. The white man said, "For three months after that revival, I suffered awful turmoil before God spoke to my soul and gave me peace."

"I know what you mean," replied the black man. "I went through the same thing for nearly two weeks."

The white man was somewhat disturbed. "Why did God speak to you so much sooner than he did to me?"

The black man answered kindly, "The reason is that you white folk have so much clothing upon you. When Christ calls, you cannot run to him. But we poor colored folk have only one ragged coat. When we hear His call, we can throw it off instantly and run to Him."

C. But, then, that was during the days of slavery in this country. Today, many blacks, along with whites, would have to throw off too many outer garments to run to Jesus as did Bartimaeus. Permit me to mention a few: our pseudo-sophistication; our cynical view of Christianity and the established church; our secular preoccupation with material security; our abstract theory and secular philosophy; our skepticism and our cynicism. Our doubts, fears, and distrust; the list is endless.

Point Two

Jesus saw Bartimaeus' need and Jesus cared.

And He cares about those of us who are sitting by the road as well. Well, I hear a skeptic say, "This world is so big, how could I possibly believe that God cares about me?" "When I consider the vastness of creation, over 600 million miles across, over 200 billion stars, and the sun and the moon shining in their splendor, "What is man that thou art mindful of him?" (Psalm 8:2). Important questions.

Well, Harry Emerson Fosdick dealt with this question many years ago in his book, *The Meaning of Prayer.* This great preacher and scholar reminded us that we do not judge the value of a thing on the basis of size. While we were yet children we learned that a dime has more value than a nickel, even though the nickel is larger. We can dig up a two-ton rock out of the ground and it will not be as valuable as a small diamond.

A. In other words, we do not judge value on the basis of size. Neither does God. We may be a very tiny part of God's creation, but every bit of evidence from both theology and science supports the proposition that this world was created on our behalf.

B. But, you say, there are so many of us for God to love. There are over three billion people alive on earth right now. How could God know and care about each of us as individuals? Is God like the old woman who lived in the shoe, who had so many children she didn't know what to do?

Well, Dr. Fosdick helps us here as well. He reminds us that the more you know about any subject, the less you think in terms of the general, and more in terms of the specific.

1. For example: Most of us know absolutely nothing about modern-day automobiles — that is, what goes on under the hood. Suppose we own a large luxury car loaded with all kinds of options—power steering, power brakes, air conditioning, cruise control, and so on. Suppose then, for some reason, our car stops on a lonely, deserted road. We throw open the hood of the car. What do we see? If we are not familiar with what goes on under the hood of a car, chances are that all we will see will be a mass of metal, rubber hoses, belts, and wires. Just a meaningless mass, a blob, if you please.

We throw up our hands in utter disgust and have our car towed to the garage. The mechanic at the garage looks under the hood, but he doesn't see a blob. He sees the distributor cap and the alternator and fuel pump. He reaches around the carburetor and tightens a little nut that is not even visible to us, gives us a big bill, and sends us on our way.

You see, the more you know about cars, the more you think in terms of the individual parts of a car and the less you think in terms of the car as a whole.

2. Consider another example: Suppose you and I were to travel to China—that great nation of more than one billion people. We go downtown, and it is rush hour. Thousands of busy people are jostling through the streets. What is likely to be our first impression? What will we see? Probably we will just see a great mass of yellow faces.

Now I don't want to offend anyone this morning, but, do you know the greatest statement of ignorance is? The greatest statement of ignorance is: "They all look the same to me."

If we were to stay awhile among the Chinese and were to grow to know and love individual Chinese persons, no longer would they all look the same to us. We would see them as individuals.

3. Listen: God knows every Chinese by name. God knows every Israeli and Palestinian by name. God knows every boy and girl in South Africa by name. Even the hairs on our heads are numbered. In other words, God does not see us simply as a sea of humanity. He sees us and loves us as individual persons. Hallelujah!

Point Three

Jesus saw blind Bartimaeus and cared about the poor beggar's blindness.

He called for Bartimaeus to come to Him. Bartimaeus responded eagerly. He cast off his garment and came to Jesus.

"What wilt thou that I should do unto you?", Jesus asks him.

"Lord, that I might receive my sight", replies Bartimaeus.

"Go thy way", says Jesus, "thy faith hath made thee whole."

Listen: Those of us who are sitting by the side of the road begging—waiting for someone to help us out of our dilemma, our faith can make us well.

If you can believe that the God of this vast universe cares about your needs and will see you through whatever crisis you may be confronting, then cast aside your garment. Cast aside your stubborn pride, cast aside your conceit, cast aside individualism, cast aside egotism, cast aside your snobbishness, cast aside self-opinions:

"Why should I feel discouraged, why should the shadows come;
Why should my heart feel lonely, and long for heaven and home?
When Jesus is my portion, my constant friend is He,
His eye is on the sparrow, and I know He watches me!

I sing because I'm happy, I sing because I'm free
His eye is on the sparrow and I know He watches me!"

THE DOORKEEPER'S SONG

"For a day in thy courts is better than a thousand. I had rather be a doorkeeper in the house of my God, than to dwell in the tents of wickedness" (Psalm 84:10).

INTRODUCTION

If one were to state in general terms the principal thought that underlies this text, it would be this: that life must be measured by quality as well as by quantity.

One day may be better than a thousand, just as a single gold coin is better than a handful of copper. A day of liberty is better than a thousand years in a prison. A day of good health is worth many days of sickness.

A life lived among the comforts and blessings of civilization is richer and fuller than a life of ignorance and barbarism. If we had our choice we would say, "There is no comparison. A day is better than a thousand of the other."

A certain recording artist once said (his name escapes me at the moment), "I'd trade a lifetime for just one day in paradise."

Take the lives of two men, for example. They may be equal in length, but most unequal in value. Their days may be the same in number, but not the same in preciousness.

As David's men said to him when he was preparing to go forth to battle with them against his son, Absalom, "Thou shalt not go forth; thou art worth ten thousand of us" (2 Samuel 18:3).

Even so we find—the life of one man priceless, of another, practically worthless—so that one day is better than a thousand, more beautiful, more fruitful, more enduring.

It is in this context that the psalmist says, "A day in thy courts is better than a thousand." Someone once said, and I agree, "The worst Christian of Christ is better than the best sinner."

To be a doorkeeper in God's house is preferable to the softest seat or the most exalted place among the wicked. Alvin Barkley, the late Vice President of the United States, once stated, "I would rather be a doorkeeper in the house of the Lord, than to sit in the seat of the mighty."

Satan teaches for a doctrine that it is better to reign in hell than to serve in heaven. He would have men to believe that God's service is a bondage and that God's house is a place of weariness and gloom.

I hereby refute that devilish doctrine. In fact, I call him a liar, yea, the father of lies. For life apart from God is poor and worthless, lacking the quality of true life. There is no glory in it, no immortal hope. Therefore, it is fitly compared to the life of the blind or the state of the dead, for tried by the highest standard, it is no life at all.

It is the life spent in God's service that is alone worth living and incomparably the best. The psalmist, then, had a true sense of relative values when he said, "I had rather be a doorkeeper in the house of my God, than to dwell in the tents of wickedness."

I. Various reasons might be given in support of this opinion. Consider, for one thing, the dignity of God's service. It is the service of the Most High God. It brings us into the presence of Him who is King of kings and Lord of lords.

In many foreign lands today, where the monarchy is still the accepted form of government, people count it an honor to serve the king. Such service confers an honor and dignity upon them that rank and fortune can give. People eagerly covet any office that will bring them into the king's presence and into the royal household. They would rather that than have a score of servants at their beck and call.

In this, we see the spirit of the psalmist in a more ignoble form. Better to serve in the king's house than to be served and honored anywhere else. When Sir Walter Raleigh spread his new cloak in the dust for Queen Elizabeth to walk over, he was really saying, "Better to be walked on by you than worn by a subject."

What shall we, then, say of the service of Him before whom all earthly kings must bend the knee? Surely, no greater honor could be conferred upon a man than to serve, even in the smallest capacity, for Him who is King of kings and Lord of lords.

A number of years ago, through the medium of television, I witnessed the coronation of Queen Elizabeth of Great Britain, and what a magnificent, impressive ceremony it was. After all of the pomp and circumstance, the ceremony culminated in a solemn and beautiful act that pointed to a higher realm. When the crown had been placed on her head she, in turn, knelt at the altar, pledging herself to the service of God—that she would seek divine assistance in the task of governing her people.

That act, to me, says that God's service is higher than the highest earthly dignities. The greatest gifts and talents, the highest power of intellect and of heart are glorified when they are employed in God's service. In any lower service, they are misspent and flung away. It would be well for each of us to always bear this in mind—that God's service is the noblest work we can ever be called upon to do.

Christian people are contented, oftentimes, to give what's left of their time to God; what's left of their strength and the loose coins of their income, under the impression, seemingly, that they can use their powers and talents to better purpose otherwise, and that the mere ends and sweepings are good enough for God.

Such service is an insult to our King. We can never be better employed than in His service. The psalmist felt it was an honor to do the humblest thing for God. To be a doorkeeper was perhaps a lowly office, but, then, it was God's house, and that made all the difference.

Several years ago, I was commending one of the senior members of the church for his Christ-like spirit in which he relinquished his position, so that a younger member might have an opportunity to display his talent and ability: "Any capacity in which I might be called upon to serve is good enough for me. If no other capacity, I'll be satisfied to be the janitor."

There, I later thought, spoke reverence and the true spirit of service. We may not be able to do anything great in itself, or occupy a place of prominence, but if we bear in mind that it is God's service—if we say to ourselves continually, "I do this for God," then we shall realize that there is dignity in the service of the King, and we shall feel ourselves honored in the doing of it.

II. Consider further that God's service is to be preferred because of its permanence. The psalmist seems to point to this when he contrasts the "house of God" with the "tents of wickedness."

A house has foundation and stands year after year, and from generation to generation. The tent is movable and shifting—here today and gone tomorrow.

By this we are reminded that the pleasures of sin are but for a season. They that dwell in the tents of wickedness shall one day be left destitute. But the humblest servant of God will always have a roof above his head, a shelter from the storm, a refuge in the time of trouble, and a dwelling place forever.

This was the psalmist's confidence: "The Lord God", he says, "is a sun and shield. The Lord will give grace and glory, and he will be our guide, even unto death" (Psalm 84:11). This is what he had reference to when he said, "Surely goodness and mercy shall follow me all the days of my life; and I will dwell in the house of the Lord forever" (Psalm 23:6).

III. Finally, God's service is to be preferred because it is a service of love: "Better a dinner of herbs where love is," says the wise man Solomon, "than a stalled ox and hatred therewith" (Proverbs 15:17), along with "Better a thy crust [of bread] and with it peace than a house where feast and dispute go together" (Proverbs 17:1).

Better to dwell in the abode of love than to frequent the haunts of sin, where lust and selfishness and falsehood are. Better a doorkeeper in the father's house than to be exalted among the wicked, amid envy and strife.

Plainly, the psalmist prefers God's house and God's service because his heart is there. He says, "A single day spent in your temple is better than a thousand anywhere else. I would rather be a doorman of the temple of God than live in palaces of wickedness." And, again, he says, "I was glad", not sad, not melancholy, not cast down in spirit, but "I was glad when they said unto me, Let us go into the house of the Lord."

"Only to stand on the threshold, though I see not the Master's face—
At the gate of His holy place to have my name and my place;
From my post I shall never wander, at my watch I shall never sleep,
And my heart shall sing for gladness at the door I am set to keep.

Only to stand on the threshold, alas! This were heaven to me,
After the dreary desert, after the wintry sea;
But! hear Him call me higher, in accents low and sweet
I shall not stand on the threshold, but stand at the Master's feet—James H. Morrison.

When the humble doorkeeper shall hear the voice which bids him, "Come up higher," he shall exchange the threshold for the throne. For the Master has declared that "To him that overcometh will I grant to sit with me in my throne, even as I have overcome, and am set down with my Father in His throne" (Revelation 3:21).

First Baptist Church, Finleyville, PA, where my grandfather served from 1947-1949 and my uncle served from 1953-1967

Trinity Baptist Church, Pittsburgh, PA, where my grandfather served from 1949-1964

Vermont Baptist Church, Creighton, PA, where Rev. A. L. Wingfield served from 1967-1993

Mt. Olive Baptist Church in Sharpsburg, PA, where my father served from 1965-1973

Second Baptist Church, Farrell, PA, where my father served from 1973-1982

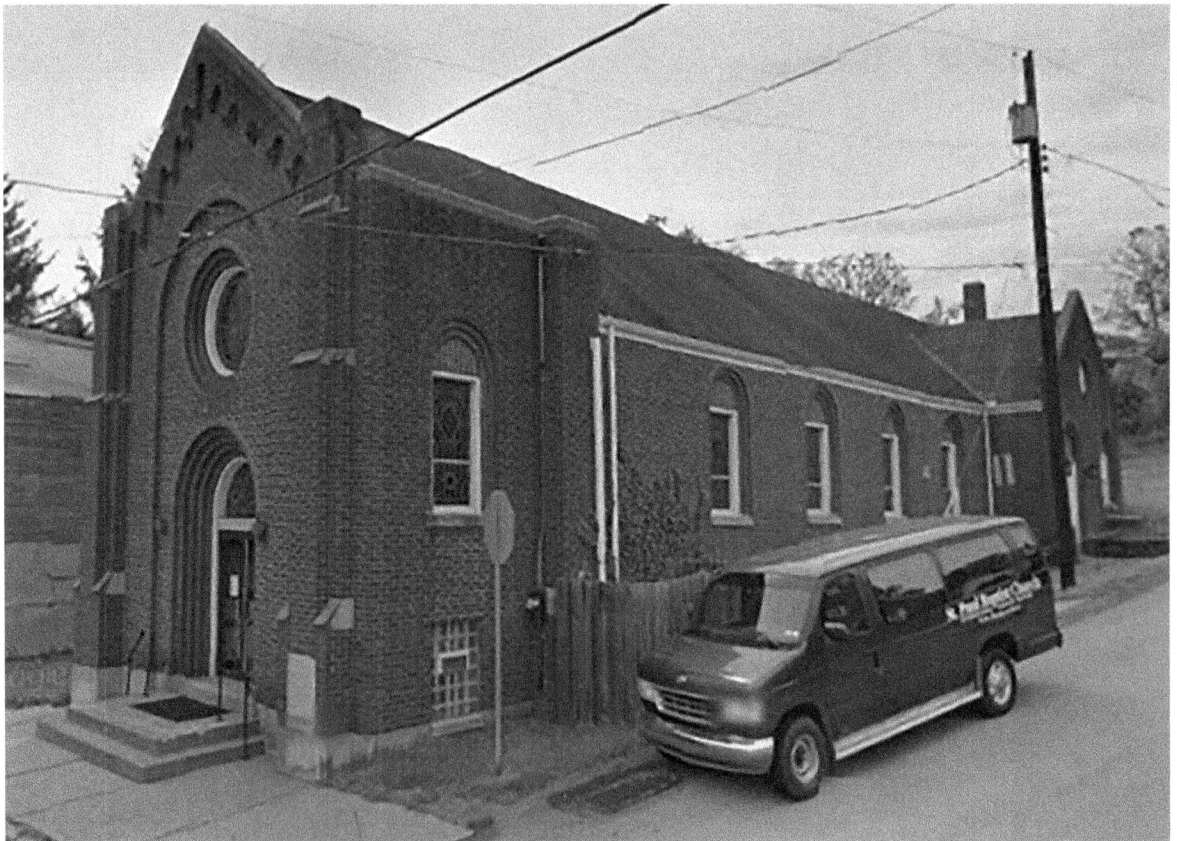

St. Paul Baptist Church, Donora, PA, where I served from 1989-1997

Bethel Baptist Church, Braddock, PA, where I served from 1997-2003

Unity Baptist Church, Braddock, PA, where I have served from 2004 to present

SECTION THREE
REV. W. W. WINGFIELD, JR.

Reverend W. W. Wingfield, Jr., my father, continued the tradition of preaching within the family. Born in Bluefield, West Virginia on April 14, 1927, he was educated in the Pittsburgh Public School District. After his call to the ministry, he continued his education and received a diploma in theology through the Baptist Institute of Christian Service, an extension of the American Baptist Theological Seminary.

Following the death of his father, Reverend Wingfield accepted the call to the gospel ministry, preaching his initial sermon on January 17, 1965 at Trinity Baptist Church. Six months later, he was called to pastor Mt. Olive Baptist Church in Sharpsburg, Pennsylvania. His pastorate began on July 4, 1965. He was instrumental in leading this congregation in the building of an ultra-modern facility.

In May of 1973, he was called to pastor the Second Baptist Church of Farrell, Pennsylvania. Among his many accomplishments there, he led the congregation in an extensive renovation program of its facility. His civic activities included secretary-treasurer of the Farrell-Wheatland Ministerial Association, Vice President of the Mercer County Urban League, former auditor of the Eastern Ohio Western Pennsylvania Association, and a board member of the Mercer County NAACP.

After seventeen years of ministry, Reverend Wingfield died suddenly on April 28, 1982 while enjoying a game of golf with friends.

THE CONTEXT

W. W. Wingfield, Jr. preached during a time of social upheaval. Race riots were prevalent throughout the nation. Within the span of two months, the nation had witnessed the assassinations of Martin Luther King, Jr., and Robert F. Kennedy, causing violence to break out in major metropolitan areas. The close of the 1960s set the stage for a decline in the Black revolution.

Black consciousness was on the rise. Blacks were beginning to make gains politically, socially and economically. Although there were some who benefited from the "Great Society," the masses were still very much estranged from the mainstream of American life. The decade of the 1970s witnessed high unemployment, street violence, drug addiction, and a gradual decline of the Black church and family,

In the midst of this mix, W. W. Wingfield, Jr. spoke prophetically. He sounded the alarm and challenged his hearers about becoming stagnant and warned them about forgetting the God who brought them through.

Reverend Wingfield was theologically conservative and politically moderate. He was progressively-minded and had a passion for the progress and elevation of Blacks nationwide. Thus, he believed and preached a message of liberation, though he did not ascribe to all the tenets of Black liberation theology.

For the most part, he was a flat-footed preacher, though he was known to leave his pulpit on certain occasions in order to stress his point.

ANSWERS FOR A WORLD IN TROUBLE[b]

"Then Zedekiah, the king, sent and took him out: And the king asked him secretly in his house, and said, 'Is there any word from the Lord?' And Jeremiah said, 'There is. . .'" (Jeremiah 37:17).

This past summer our nation experienced some very difficult and dark days from which tension is still mounting today. It had to undergo riots in at least two of its major cities and the threat of riots in others. These riots produced some results worthy of consideration by all rational minded and sensible thinking people of our day. It is sad to say, but it took a near revolution to convince the power structure of this country to seek a solution to the social and economic problems that have plagued the people of our race for so many years.

I feel it necessary to say, however, that we did not condone the actions of those who participated in the riots. For we consider their acts to be a hindrance rather than a help to the cause for which we are fighting. But, thanks be to God, somebody is seeking a solution.

One of the results of the riots is the awakening of the people to the fact that the world is in trouble. These earth-shaking events have aroused the conscience of many people who are no longer content to sit smugly at home and occasionally express a concern for the underprivileged people of the world. They are ready now to do something about existing conditions.

The nation has been shaken out of a state of complacency. It knows now that when a usually non-violent people take a gun in hand to destroy and kill, and cause millions of dollars of damage by burning and looting, and are willing to die, if necessary, for the cause they profess, it can draw no other conclusion than that the world is in trouble. When the nation discovered the results that come out of the Black Power conference in New Jersey following the riots there, where separation of races was advocated, plus a strong anti-white and anti-Christian tone was stressed, it had to know that it meant trouble for the world.

It knows now that any time a nation of people or a race of people will go contrary to the way God has designed for them to live, the world is in trouble. And may I add, regardless of what their reasons are, they may be an oppressed people or they may have been denied their rights, but when they go contrary to the will of God, the world is in trouble.

The difficulty we have experienced, and are experiencing, cannot be resolved in a day, or a week, or a month, or even a year. It takes time for wounds to heal such as has been inflicted upon some people. Therefore, I feel that the world is in trouble.

However, I feel advised to caution us by saying that no group of people needs to sit back and gloat or take pride in what is happening in our land today. As members of the oppressed race, we can be thankful that a solution to our problems is being sought, but we have no right to take pride in the way it came about. For when the world is in trouble, everyone is in trouble. I don't care what color

---

[b]This sermon was preached at Central Baptist Church in Pittsburgh on December, 1967, during the racial struggles of this era in various cities across the nation, including Pittsburgh.

they may be: black, white, yellow, green or blue, when the world is in trouble, everyone is in trouble.

There riots have no meaningful purpose, and they are nothing to be proud of. They are instigated and participated in mostly by the unruly element of our society. A few innocents have fallen victim to their teaching but the damage is done by the radical and the extremist among us, all under the banner of the cause.

But (listen), they will just as quickly burn and loot your and my place of business, and our homes, and dispossess us of our goods as well as the next man's. There is no such thing as a soul brother as far as the looters are concerned. If they think you have something of value and can get away with it, they will take our belongings too. (Listen) The world is in trouble, not just a few folks, not just one race of people, but the world is in trouble.

(I'm not asking anyone to agree with me, I simply want you to think about it. We're in trouble. Before this situation runs its course, everyone will be made aware of it).

Another result that comes out of the strife that exists in our land is the recognition of the Church and its role in bringing men to an understanding. The Church has been asked to help, and rightfully so, for this is our business. But unfortunately, there are those who would like nothing better for the church to take a middle-of-the-road stand, not only on this issue, but on all issues. When men in authority, however, in high positions in government and industry, realize the importance of the Church even in matters of state, it is a step in the right direction.

A few months ago, the President of this nation proclaimed a day of prayer and urged all citizens to attend the church of his or her choice, to pray for peace and friendship among men of all races. We were in accord with this action, and we commend the President for taking it. We also commend those who complied with his request.

But I want to remind us that prayer should be a continual effort on the part of all Christians. "Men ought to always pray and not to faint" (Luke 18:1). We ought to include in our prayers a desire for peace in the land and that the differences between the races would soon be resolved.

I want to remind us also that the Christian's duty after prayer is to get up and do something about the conditions for which he is praying. Our obligation does not end in simply praying. It is only the beginning.

I cannot help but feel that God does not care too much about doing for us what we can do for ourselves. I believe that He expects or requires us to exhaust the limit of our abilities in matters like this and, after we have done all that we can do, then call on Him for help.

With this thought in mind, every Christian in America today ought to get busy and start praying and working to help put an end to the current situation, for the nation is eagerly awaiting the outcome of our prayers.

The world is in trouble now and leaders realize it. They are trying daily to work things out to satisfaction of all concerned. They have organized the Peace Corps, they have instituted the poverty program, they have allocated money for rent supplement, free food stamps, Medicare, and many other programs that time will fail me to mention.

But thus far, everything tried has proved to be of little help and instead of things getting better, they seem to be getting worse.

They have come to the place now where they recognize that help is needed from a higher source. Thus, they have appealed to the Church. And there is a strong possibility that in the very near future, the leaders of our nation will seek out the hierarchy of the Church and anxiously ask the question, "Is there any word from the Lord"? And can we look for help from His direction?

Isn't it tragic that the world never thinks of God until trouble comes? Isn't it tragic that the world never thinks of God until it comes face to face with trouble? Isn't it tragic? It is tragic because it has been given every opportunity to seek God in the time of peace and tranquility. Yet, it never takes advantage of His willingness to lead, guide, and direct the lives of men until trouble stares it in the face. Isn't it tragic?

This is also true in the lives of individuals. We are given opportunity after opportunity to seek the Lord while He may be found and to call upon Him while He is near, but we never take advantage of the invitation. We ignore the plea altogether until we are plagued with difficulty and trouble and come to our wit's end and don't know what to do. It is then that we turn to the Church to seek God's help and advice.

This is the gist of the story surrounding the text today. The people of Judah led by King Zedekiah were facing a situation similar to the one we are facing today. Although he, his advisors, and the people of the land did not hearken unto the word of the Lord, Zedekiah, nevertheless, sought the prayers of the prophet Jeremiah to halt the approaching calamity facing the nation.

You will discover in reading this chapter that Zedekiah's actions illustrate the common practice of people who will fly to the protection of religion when trouble comes, although they neglect all its obligations of holiness and service.

I want to let the world know that religion requires obedience to God's will. I want to let the world know that religion is not a one-sided affair. For God speaks words of command, as well as, words of consolation, and it becomes our duty to hear and obey.

I want to let the world know that prayer without obedience is vain. God does not expect our lives to be spotless before He will answer our prayers, but, He does require that we repent of our past disobedience and show a willingness to obey Him in the future.

My hearers, as long as we remain unchanged in our conduct, we need not look for help from God, but when we turn from our sins, we can ask what we will and God will grant it.

Yes, when we turn from our sins, we can look to God for help despite the fact that we have shut him out of our lives and, in many instances, forbidden His followers to speak His name in public gatherings.

Despite the fact that in some areas, we no longer permit our children to call on His name in prayer in public schools, we can look to God for help. For He is a forgiving God, He is a merciful God: "Though your sins be as scarlet," he said, "I'll make them white as snow" (Isaiah 1:18).

Although the world is waiting to hear from God, it may be of interest to know that His answers were recorded in a book that we call the Bible, and they are here for all to read. This book has served as a guide to mankind for generations and will continue to serve for generations to come.

Listen to God's answer to the Black Power advocates who would take the country by force. It is recorded in Zechariah 4:6, and it reads, "Not by might, nor by power, but by my spirit, saith the Lord."

His answer to our nation's leaders is recorded in 2 Chronicles 7:14, and it reads, "If my people, which are called by my name, shall humble themselves and pray, and seek my face, and turn from their wicked ways, then will I hear from heaven, and will forgive their sin and heal their land."

Listen, "Let the wicked forsake his way, and the unrighteous man his thoughts, and let him return unto the Lord, and he will abundantly pardon" (Isaiah 55:7). "Trust in the Lord and do good, so shalt thy dwell in the land and verily thou shalt be fed" (Psalm 37:3).

Listen. "Trust in the Lord with all thine heart, and lean not unto thy own understanding. In all thy ways acknowledge him, and he shall direct thy path" (Proverbs 3:5). "Blessed is the man that walketh not in the counsel of the ungodly, nor standeth in the way of sinners, nor sitteth in the seat of the scornful" (Psalm 1:1).

THE PROBLEM AND THE CURE[7]

**"Is there no balm in Gilead? Is there no physician there?
Why then is not the health of the daughter of my people recovered?" (Jeremiah 8:22).**

The problem is not just that twenty-one black children have been slain in Atlanta, Georgia. Lest we forget, murder occurs on a daily basis in this nation and mass murder has occurred in several cities in recent years.

No, the problem is deeper than that. This problem can be traced back to the early days of this nation's history when certain conditions prevailed and were allowed to remain unchecked. I would like to mention just a few of those conditions and also mention a few others that have developed in recent years.

- Hate, the most destructive of them all;
- Injustice, the cruelest of them all;
- Apathy, the most distasteful;
- Exploitation, the most vicious;
- Segregation, the most immoral;
- The denial of human rights, the most spiteful;
- Double standard, the most malicious;
- Bigotry, prejudice, jealousy, greediness, immorality, homosexuality, drug abuse, alcoholism—wickedness in high places.

I could go on.

These sickening conditions, like a cancer, have spread throughout the length and breadth of this nation, and have affected every man, woman, and child, directly or indirectly. Now, any doctor will tell you that if a cancer is allowed to go unchecked, it will continue to eat away at the body until that whole body is infected and destroyed.

That's the problem facing this nation today: Destructive, cancerous conditions have been tolerated by this society, yea, even in some cases, sanctioned. And now it has come to the surface.

To put it another way, we are living in a sick society. And the symptoms of this sickness are most apparent in the horrible and senseless murders that we have witnessed in places like Atlanta, Buffalo, Chicago, and elsewhere in this nation.

It appears to me that we have come to the place described in the first chapter of the prophecy of Isaiah, written some seven hundred and sixty years before the birth of Christ. That's a long time ago, in case you don't realize it. Despite that fact, however, we need to examine that passage. For it appears as if the prophet is speaking directly at our time and to our situation. Listen to what he says in verses four to six:

---

[7]This sermon was preached as part of a community prayer vigil held at the Second Baptist Church of Farrell, Pennsylvania in response to the killing of several children in Atlanta, Georgia.

"Ali sinful nation, a people laden with iniquity, a seed of evildoers,
children that are corrupt. They have forsaken the Lord,
they have provoked the Holy One of Israel unto anger,
they are gone away backward" (Isaiah 1:4).

The prophet continues with this devastating message:

"The whole head is sick, and the whole heart faint.
From the sole of the foot even unto the head,
there is no soundness in it; but wounds, and bruises
and putrefying sores: they have not been closed,
neither bound up, neither mollified with ointment" (Isaiah 1:6).

Now, there is certainly a strong similarity between the situation the prophet speaks of and the situation we are facing in this nation. In both cases, the sickness has reached epidemic proportion. In both cases, the sickness is widespread. And, in both cases, no attempt has been made to arrest the disease.

Now, that's a tragic position for a nation to find itself. For any time conditions, like the ones mentioned here, exist within a nation's borders, that nation is headed for trouble and destined for destruction. That could be what we are headed for in this country. We could well be inviting disaster or signing our own death warrant if we fail to do something about the existing conditions.

There is a popular phrase of some years ago that says, "when an irresistible force meets an immovable object, something has got to give." If we let things continue on in the same old fashion, if we continue with business as usual, we might find ourselves in a world of trouble.

Now, I don't say these things to alarm anyone and I don't want anyone to think that all is lost, for there is a bright side to all of this. As serious as this is, the situation is not hopeless. *There is a cure for the nation's ills.* Any doctor will tell you that the vast majority of illnesses can either be arrested or cured. So it is in this case.

The Cure

To arrest or cure the disease that plagues us, first of all, we must recognize the fact that it is sick. You see, a lot of people in this country are sick and don't know it. Others know it, but refuse to admit it.

That's a sad commentary, I know, but I see evidence of it almost every day. Just a few years ago, I overheard a conversation concerning the shooting of the president and someone made this statement during the conversation, "I hope he dies."

That's an awful thing to think, let alone say. But from it, we can get a glimpse of the unhealthy attitude possessed by a good percentage of the nation's population. Some people think some awful thoughts and do some awful things. Now that's an indication of sickness. Listen again to the prophet speak,

"The whole head is sick, the whole heart faint;
from the sole of the foot even to the head, there is
no soundness in it" (Isaiah 1:6).

Let me take a moment to give a few examples of how sickness can be detected:

- When you hate without a cause, you're sick.
- When you show a lack of concern or sympathy for people in trouble, you're sick.
- If you think yourself superior to any man, you're sick.
- When you are blinded by prejudice and judge a person by the color of his skin rather than by the content of his character, you're sick.
- When you allow bitterness, envy, and bigotry to control your conduct, you're sick.

One of the tragic features of this society is that a lot of people let the likes of the television character, Archie Bunker, set the pattern for their behavior as opposed to the likes of Daddy King (Rev. Martin Luther King, Sr.). Let me take a moment to tell you about Daddy King—you already know about Archie Bunker.

After the brutal murder of Martin, Jr., the son in whom he delighted, Daddy King sat in his pulpit one Sunday morning and witnessed the senseless murder of his wife while she was playing the organ for the service. Following that tragic experience, Daddy King, in his first public appearance on television, made the statement, "I don't care what happens, I ain't gonna let nobody drag me low enough to hate him."

Now that was a tremendous statement to make. I wonder what the Archie Bunkers of this nation would have said in a similar situation? Friends, there can be no cure for our illness until the diagnosis is recognized and accepted.

Second, to cure this devastating disease, the nation must also recognize that there is a remedy. that the problem *can* be adequately dealt with.

Now, I don't propose to tell you what the government can do or what course civic leaders should follow. I want to let you know what a nation under God can do. A few centuries ago, a concerned prophet raised these questions in a faltering nation, "Is there no balm in Gilead? Is there no physician there? Why, then, has the health of the daughter of my people not been restored?" (Jeremiah 8:22).

Friends, I have come to tell you tonight that there is a prescription for the ills of this nation. There is a balm. I hear the answers coming directly from the mouth of God himself. Listen to him:

> "If my people, which are called by my name, will humble
> themselves and pray, and seek my face, and turn from their
> wicked ways, I will hear from heaven, I will forgive their
> sin and will heal their land" (2 Chronicles 7:14).

I hear these words also:

> "Return unto me, and I will return unto you,
> saith the Lord." Let the wicked forsake his way, and the
> unrighteous man his thoughts; and let him return unto
> the Lord, and he will have mercy upon him,
> for he will abundantly pardon" (Zechariah 1:3).

Yes, there is a balm in Gilead to make the wounded whole; there is a balm in Gilead to heal the sin sick soul. When you go out from here tonight, spread the news. Tell your friends and neighbors. Tell the world. There is a balm in Gilead!

THE BURNING BUSH

**"Now Moses kept the flock of Jethro his father-in-law, the priest of Midian:
and he led the flock to the backside of the desert, and came to the mountain of God,
even to Horeb. . . And Moses said, I will now turn aside, and see this great sight,
why the bush is not burnt" (Exodus 3:1-3).**

It isn't unusual to see a brush fire in desert country or wilderness. In fact, it is a common thing when the sun is hot and the atmosphere is dry, sometimes a whole hillside will burst into flames. But a burning bush not consumed—or not burning up—is something different. That's unusual, a strange and phenomenal sight. Something unheard of—mysterious—fascinating. Moses, intrigued by this strange sight—a bush on fire and not consumed, said, "I'll turn aside and see this great sight—why the bush is not burned.

The burning-bush experience made a drastic change in the life of Moses. Before seeing that sight, he was a keeper of sheep, a shepherd employed by his father-in-law, a job with no future and of little significance—unworthy of his ability and talents.

But afterwards, his life took on new meaning. For God spoke to him out of the midst of that bush and gave him a new job—a job worthy of his talents, one in which he could put to use all of the knowledge and expertise he had acquired. This new assignment came about because of one thing. He turned aside to see what was happening to the bush. His attention was attracted—his curiosity was aroused.

Of course, God set that bush on fire for that very purpose—that he might get Moses' attention and [get him] started on the task that he had prepared him for. God raised Moses up for the specific task of delivering the people of Israel from bondage in Egypt. When he was first born, his life was spared. While other male children his age were put to death at the command of Pharaoh, God fixed it so that Moses was brought up right in Pharaoh's palace as the son of his daughter who fished him out of the bulrushes where his mother had hidden him.

Later, when he was old enough to understand and see the cruelty inflicted upon his people by the Egyptians, he left Egypt because he slew an Egyptian who was mistreating one of the Hebrew brothers. From there, he fled to the wilderness where he met Jethro, a priest of Midian, and married one of his daughters, and settled down to raise his family forgetting about the plight of his people in Egypt.

But now, God was ready to move and deliver Israel from the awesome burden of slavery and give them the land that he promised to their ancestors, Abraham, Isaac, and Jacob.

So, while Moses was tending sheep one day out on the backside of the desert, God set a bush on fire, but took the heat out of the flames so that the bush would burn but not burn up. When Moses saw the bush aflame but not consumed, his curiosity was aroused and he stopped to investigate.

Now, stopping to investigate that phenomenon made Moses a special kind of man in the sight of God. The kind of man that God could use and work with and work through. God can't use every person, for some people can witness a strange sight, such as a burning bush that is not consumed, and walk on by as if nothing is happening. They can look upon a strange phenomenal sight and think nothing of it—and go about their daily routine undisturbed and unmoved.

It's hard to attract people's attention, and get them interested in anything other than the daily routine of ordinary things. Today, most people are concerned only with earning their daily bread and they could care less about what's going on around them.

We have witnessed some strange happenings in our day, some history-making events, and yet very few people have been moved to turn side and examine them. For example, we have seen a president, a senator, and several renowned civil rights leaders murdered in cold blood, and, for the most part, the only thing that has been said or done by the general public is to express regret at the tragedy of the events.

Very few, if any, have looked beyond the tragic aspect for some kind of answer to the dilemma facing us. It just seems like nobody cares if the criminal element rules the world. For the most part, we are sitting idly by, every man under his own vine and fig tree, while the drug pusher and unruly element control our lives, ruin the lives of our kids, and corrupt our government officials with large sums of money.

Where is that person who will turn aside and see or investigate these strange happenings? A lot of people are so complacent about things like this that they won't go out to vote.

What most people don't realize is that crime in the streets is a burning bush. Corruption is a burning bush. Watergates are burning bushes. And the only answer is that we turn aside and investigate it and do something about it. Our salvation depends on whether or not we turn aside.

I don't know, but it seems to me that the logical thing for us to do in situations like these is ask the questions, "What can I do? How can I help? What steps can I take?"

One of the tragic mistakes men make and have made down through the centuries is passing the buck: "Let John do it." Shirking responsibility. Relying upon somebody else to solve all the problems or make all the decisions.

You know, that's the biggest problem facing the church. Very few are willing to make the sacrifice. Very few want to assume any responsibility. "Let John do it." While we watch our favorite television program or while we run down to the club every evening. In the meantime, the Church is losing its power and influence.

Very few are willing to turn aside. That's a strange thing because when we pray, we ask the Lord to bless our church, bless our community, get rid of all the bad influences, make our streets safe. We ask the Lord to do it when we have within our power the wherewithall to answer our own prayers. But we don't want to turn aside. We don't want to stick our necks out. We don't want to make the sacrifice.

But things are not going to get better until we recognize the seriousness of the situation and be willing to do something about it.

Well, what can we do and how can we bring about the needed changes?

First of all, we can wake up out of our sleep. We can stop being complacent. We can show some concern. We can turn aside. That's all we need to do. The Lord will take it from there.

When Moses turned aside to examine that burning bush, God spoke to him out of the midst of it and revealed unto him His plan for the deliverance of Israel: "I've got some people in Egypt in bondage and I need somebody to go down and speak to Pharaoh on their behalf and demonstrate my power to him."

"You just go down and speak to him and I'll do the rest. Open your mouth and I'll speak for you. I'll persuade him. I'll tell you what to do, when to do, and how to do. You just go down."

That's all God wants. Somebody who is concerned, somebody with courage and faith enough to trust Him and let Him work through them.

Go preach My gospel, saith the Lord,
Bid the whole earth My grace receive;
He shall be saved that trust My word,
And be concerned who'll not believe.

I'll make your Great Commission known,
And you shall prove My gospel true;
By all the works that I have done,
And by all the wonders you shall do.

Teach all the nations My command,
I'm with you till the world shall end,
All power entrusted in My hands,
I can destroy, I can defend.

Because Moses accepted God's challenge, God not only delivered Israel, but He also made a new man out of Moses. Instead of a sheep-herder, he became known as a deliverer, as a builder of nations. God brought him out of obscurity in the wilderness and made him a prince among men all because he turned aside.

He's done the same with other great men. He gave Elijah the power to stand before Jezebel and Ahab one day and declared, "There will be no rain in the land except according to my word."

He gave David the power and courage to stand before Goliath and say, "You come to me with a sword, but I come to you in the name of the Lord God of Israel."

He enabled Daniel to spend a night in a den of lions and the Hebrew boys to walk courageously in the fiery furnace.

I heard the voice of Jesus say,
Come unto me and rest.
Lay down thy weary one lay down,
Thy head upon My breast.

I came to Jesus as I was,
Weary, worn and sad;
I found in Him a resting place,
And He has made me glad.

SPIRITUAL ROOTS

"And because they had no roots they withered away" (Matthew 13:6).

Much is being said about "roots" today. Alex Haley really started something when he came out with his book on the subject of *Roots*. He stirred up the desire in many people to know more about their background and who their ancestors were.

The roots fever is running high. I can't hardly get Barbara to cook these days. Every spare minute she is working on her roots. All we hear anymore is roots.

One of the things Mr. Haley discovered in the search of his roots was a high moral standard and a deep religious conviction on the part of some of his ancestors. They were not the wild, uncivilized savages that most Africans have been pictured as being.

Whether or not this knowledge had any effect upon Mr. Haley's personal life, I don't recall. However, those of us who read the book should certainly begin to think in terms of our own spiritual standing, or spiritual roots.

Black people should know and always remember that religion played a vital and important role in the survival of our ancestors. They endured the suffering and hardships that they went through, basically because they had a strong religious belief and conviction.

Dr. David Shannon of Pittsburgh Theological Seminary made a comparison of the enslavement of blacks and the enslavement of the Israelite nation. One of the things he pointed out was that when the Israelites, God's chosen people, were asked to sing to their captors one of the songs of Zion, they refused and hung their harps on a willow tree, saying, "How can we sing the Lord's song in a strange land?"

Contrary to the Israelites, Dr. Shannon goes on, the Black slaves didn't hesitate to sing in a strange land. He believed that perhaps then, more than ever, he needed to sing of and to his God. And, he dared to believe that his Lord would somehow free him from his captors.

Now, I think that is very significant—that attitude or outlook, that is. It's very significant. It is an outlook seldom possessed by people in bondage. And, it is an eye-opening thing because, through all of those trying experiences, these people, for the most part, never gave up hope. And, instead of throwing in the towel when they faced difficulties and trials, their leisure moments, or even as they labored under a heavy burden, they could be heard singing such songs as:

> "There is a balm in Gilead,
> To make the wounded hole;
> There is a balm in Gilead,
> To heal the sin-sick soul."

Can you imagine this type of outlook on the part of a slave? Doesn't it do something to you? Doesn't it make you proud to know that you are descendants of a people so strong to face depression and discouragement? Doesn't it?

You know, these old slaves left us a heritage that money can't buy. They didn't leave us a lot of material possessions such as land, money, automobiles, and relics of value. They couldn't because they didn't possess anything of value, but they left us a spiritual inheritance that is far more valuable than silver and gold.

You know, this much I have learned in my lifetime. There are situations in life in which silver and gold are of no value to us. And, there are times when spiritual possessions can do more for us than all the money in the world.

My daddy used to remind us often of that old Proverb, which says, "A good name is rather to be chosen than great riches, and loving favor rather than silver and gold" (Proverbs 22:1).

Proverbs 15:17 states another fact, fot it says, "Better is a dinner of herbs where love is than a stalled ox and hatred therewith." That means, you may not have money to buy the best foods or to eat high on the hog, but if you are in a situation where such things as love and friendship are present, you are better off than a person who spreads his lavish table in an atmosphere of hatred and bitterness.

Note: The experiences of our ancestors should make us all the more aware of our own spiritual needs. That is, their experiences should teach us that we need something more than just knowledge of where we came from and who our kinfolk were. We need, more than anything else, we need to know how we can live up to our best and highest potential.

We need to know what to do when trouble comes.

We need to know how to deal with opposition.

We need to know where to turn when we are disillusioned and discouraged.

We need to know the best answer to problems and the best solution to troubles.

We need to know how to survive in a world of confusion, hatred, conflict, and strife.

We need to know where to turn and where to get help when we need it.

Of course, this is a subject that you can't get out of books. This is a subject that you can't learn in the classroom because it's not so much a matter of what you know, but it's a matter of who you know. It's a matter of where you place your trust and confidence. J. B. Mackey understood this when he wrote the words of a hymn:

Is there anyone can help us,
One who understands our hearts,
When the thorns of life have pierced them till they bleed;
One who sympathizes with us,
Who in wondrous love imparts,
Just the very, very blessing that we need.

Is there anyone can help us,
When the load is hard to bear,
And we faint and fall beneath it in alarm;
Who in tenderness will lift us,
And the heavy burden share,
And support us with an everlasting arm.

He answers those questions saying;

Yes, there's One, only One,
the blessed, blessed Jesus, He's the One;
When afflictions press the soul, and waves of trouble roll,

And you need a friend to help you, He's the One.

Now, that's one of the lessons Jesus teaches in the parable of the sower. I know He talks about a farmer sowing seed, but actually, he deals with the subject of a spiritual foundation, or spiritual roots, if you please. Those without spiritual roots wither away and perish, expire, die, or fall by the wayside. They perish, mainly because they have no roots—nothing to fall back on in the day of trouble, nothing to sustain them and nothing to keep their hopes alive.

Jesus wasn't talking about a faraway situation in this parable. He was talking about conditions and people like we see every day, people who are spiritually dead and who are on their way to ruin because, in preparing for the future, or in not preparing for it, they build their house upon an unsure and unstable foundation. Who build their houses, as it were, upon the sand and the rains descended and the floods came and the winds blew and beat upon that house, and it fell.

The world is full of people who have built, and are building, upon the sands of good times, pleasures, and upon false ideologies. And I suspect that there are many of them around Farrell. I suspect that there are those who will call it quits and give up when they encounter real trouble. I suspect that there are those who will go off the deep end when problems mount up and discouragement comes.

Of course, there are also those who are deeply rooted, and who are on solid ground. And there are those who are anchored securely in the Lord. I know there are some of those around. There are those who will say with the prophet Habakkuk:

"Although the fig tree shall not blossom, neither shall fruit be in the vines,
the labor of the olive shall fail and the fields shall yield no meat,
the flock shall be cut off from the fold, and there shall be no herd in the stalls,
yet, I will rejoice in the Lord. I will joy in the God of my salvation" (Habakkuk 3:17-19).

That's what I mean by spiritual roots. To keep the faith when the way is dark. To keep on trusting when all seems lost. To hold on when black clouds of trouble hang heavy overhead.

That's what I mean by spiritual roots. To be able to say with Job: "I know that my redeemer liveth" (Job 19:25) and "Though he slay me, yet will I trust him" (Job 13:15).

To be able to say with Paul; "Know in whom I have believed, and am persuaded that he is able to keep that which I have committed unto him against that day. . ." (2 Timothy 1:12).

That's what I mean by spiritual roots!

THE ROAD FROM JERUSALEM TO JERICHO

"A certain man went down from Jerusalem to Jericho. . ." (Luke 10:30-37).

The road from Jerusalem to Jericho was a notoriously dangerous road. Jerusalem is 2,300 feet above sea level and Jericho is 1,300 feet below sea level, so then, in a little more than twenty miles, the road dropped 3,600 feet.

It was a narrow and rocky road with a lot of curves and hidden crevices. It was said to be an ideal hunting ground for renegades and robbers. In Jesus' day, it was called the Bloody Way. In the nineteenth century, it was still necessary to pay safety money to local sheiks before one could travel on it.

As late as the early 1930s, a traveler was warned to get home before dark if he intended to use the road because thieves were still holding up cars, robbing tourists, and escaping to the hills before the police could arrive.

When Jesus told this story, He was telling about the kind of things that were constantly happening on this road from Jerusalem to Jericho. Basically, He was saying that it was a dangerous road, unsafe to travel, and should be avoided. Of course, Jesus was trying to get another message over when He told this story. But today, I want to look at it from another point of view and explore some possibilities that few people give any thought to.

I want to begin with this question: What was that traveler doing on that road in the first place? That was a road that a person just didn't travel by himself. He knew that it was a dangerous road and about its reputation. He knew that others had fallen victim to thieves on that same road. So what was he doing out there?

Now, I'm not dipping here, and I'm not trying to get into the man's personal business. I would like to know if this man was just plain hard-headed and wouldn't listen, or if he was just one of those fools that the poet talked about, who "rushed in where angels fear to tread."

There are people like that, you know, who are reckless, foolish, who ignore danger signs, can't be told anything. People who plunge headlong into a dangerous situation with the attitude that nothing bad can happen to them. People who give no thought to the danger associated with a particular place or thing because they think they are too smart to get trapped. People who think they know all the ins and outs of every situation and who think they have some special charm to ward off danger and trouble. To such people, I say, learn a lesson from this parable - a valuable lesson, a helpful lesson.

First of all, you don't go tramping off down a road that's known to be dangerous and detrimental to your welfare. The road from Jerusalem to Jericho is symbolic of the road of life that we travel daily. So, what we are talking about here is not some theory or speculation, but life. Life with all of its problems, and our happiness and success or failure depends, largely, upon how we approach life.

One thing we learn from this parable is that we can approach life with the wrong attitude. For those who rush off down life's road with the feeling that they can do anything they are big enough to do and suffer no adverse consequences are in a world of trouble. They are in trouble with a capital "T." That kind of thinking has been responsible for the downfall and destruction of many lives.

Yet, it's tragic that some can't profit from the mistakes of others. There are still those who think they are too smart to get trapped, or, who will tell you, "I know what I am doing."

The drug scene is a good example. They say that there is no harm in that, but look how many people have been trapped by it! Look how many lives have been ruined by going down that road. The statistics are staggering.

Then there is this business of hanging out with the wrong crowd, or loafing on the street corners till all hours of the night. Look how many have been led down the road to destruction as a result of that.

Now I'm not advocating that we shut ourselves off in some corner and don't get any enjoyment out of life. I'm simply saying, "Check out the road." See where it is leading. Determine what the end result of your activity will be. Check out the road!

Another thing we should learn from the parable is that once we get in trouble or fall victim to some disaster, there aren't too many people who will sympathize with us or give us a helping hand. Most people take the attitude that it's our own fault. That was, basically, the attitude of the priest and the Levite in the parable: concern for their own safety.

And, you know, we condemn them for that, but haven't we been guilty of the same thing? Some have literally stood by and watched while a neighbor is beaten and robbed. If not that, we have stood by while a neighbor was being condemned and crucified by slanderous remarks and that's just as bad.

No, there aren't too many people who will come to your rescue when you fall. Some delight in seeing you fall.

Third, this parable really teaches us what life is all about. Life is far more complex than the average person thinks it is. It may look like a bed of roses and it may look like all peaches and cream. But, it isn't, and, it's far from it.

Life is full of ups and downs, ins and outs. It's full of disappointments and failures. Its full of discouragements and heartaches. They are all lying in wait to throw us down and strip us of our possessions, impede our progress, and hamper our growth.

But don't get excited. Don't get discouraged about that, because there is somebody who is there to pick you up where you have fallen down. There is somebody who will be there to wipe the tears from your eyes. There is somebody . . .

DON'T LET YOUR LIGHT GO OUT[8]

"And the foolish said unto the wise, 'Give us of your oil; for our lamps are gone out...'"
(Matthew 25:1-13).

Our Lord told a story one day about some young ladies who were invited to a wedding feast. There were ten of them in number, and as the story goes, five of them were wise, and five of them were foolish.

The foolish came by this description because they took their lamps to the feast, but took no oil with them, but the wise took oil in their vessels with their lamps. Well, the story says, that the bridegroom was late coming and they all slumbered and slept. At midnight, the cry went up, "Behold, the bridegroom cometh, go ye out to meet him." All the girls arose and trimmed their lamps. But the foolish had run out of oil—their lamps had gone out. They said to the wise, "Give us of your oil for our lamps are gone out."

The wise answered and said, "We can't do that. There isn't enough for us and you. But go ye, rather, to them that sell and buy for yourselves." While the foolish went to buy oil, the bridegroom came. And they that were ready went in with him to the marriage—and the door was shut.

Later, the story says, the foolish came, seeking entry, and couldn't get in for the marriage was already in progress. The story ends with these words, "Watch, therefore, for you know neither the day nor the hour wherein the Son of man cometh."

Now, there are several things about this story that I want to call to your attention today. First, is that portion of it where the foolish said to the wise, "Give us of your oil for our lamps are gone out." Out of this section I want to draw this subject: Don't let your light go out!

Light, as you know, is essential to our well-being. Without it, we would be compelled to walk in darkness...

Light dispels darkness... it enables us to see... It brightens up the way... it illumines the path. .. it keeps us from stumbling... it reveals danger... and last, but not least, it cheers us up when the way is dark.

There is nothing in the world more beautiful and satisfying than to see a light shining when the way has been dark and dreary or when the night has been long and difficult.

The second thing I want to call to your attention is the dilemma facing those five foolish girls. These young ladies were characteristic of the kind of people that need light. Notice, the Lord was careful to say that five of the girls were wise and five were foolish. And the emphasis was placed upon the foolish.

But we must not be disturbed or offended by the word *foolish*. The story didn't say that the foolish girls were bad, just foolish. It didn't say that they were uncooperative, just foolish. It didn't call them renegades or trouble makers, just foolish.

---

[8]This is the last sermon preached before his untimely death at the Greater Morris Chapel A.M.E. Church in Farrell, PA.

That word *foolish* simply means careless, unthinking, negligent, lax, unmindful, thoughtless, and reckless.

There are a lot of people in the world today who fit that description. Good-hearted, but foolish. Careless about their behavior—unthoughtful about their actions—negligent about responsibility—lax in terms of commitment—unmindful and thoughtless in terms of preparedness—and reckless in their living.

Such people are badly in need of light. Without light, they will soon lose their way and perish. Without light, their sense of direction will soon be out of balance, and they will be without hope and without a future.

And so I wanted to call this fact to your attention today, in hopes that all of us might do some thinking along these lines.

A popular songwriter wrote these words a few years ago, and I consider them very appropriate for this day and time. He wrote, "If everybody would light just one little candle, what a bright world this would be." I think that the Lord Jesus was thinking along those same lines when He said to His followers in that great and rich Sermon on the Mount, "Ye are the light of the world. You are like a city that's set on a hill that cannot be hid."

What He meant by that was those who abide in Him, the true light, are themselves light. And that His light, burning within them, should shine forth in their walk, in their tasks and in their actions. He meant that His followers are to be examples to those around them and that they are to influence, encourage, and help others to grow spiritually.

I think this can be summed up best by the Master's words to Simon Peter one day. He said to Simon, "Satan hath desired to have you that he may sift you as wheat. But I have prayed for you that your faith fail not. And, when you are converted, strengthen thy brethren" (Luke 22:32).

"When thou art converted, strengthen thy brethren." In other words, be a light. Be an example. How we need that today.

What we are emphasizing here is the necessity of keeping our lights from going out. And there are several things that should claim our attention.

First of all, if we let our lights go out, somebody will have to grope in darkness and face the possibility of losing his soul. Somebody's way will be made rougher and somebody's hills will be harder to climb. Somebody will falter along the way and won't be able to make it in. Somebody will be minus a road map and will be forced to tread the wine press alone.

If we let our lights go out, somebody will go through life undecided. Somebody will miss the road. Somebody will shed a few more tears and somebody will experience a few more disappointments. Somebody's heart will be broken and somebody's life will be doomed if we let our lights go out.

Oh, how we need more light today. The souls of men are dying and we need more light. The hosts of sin are pressing hard to draw us from the skies and we need more light. There's much sorrow in the land, much crying, much distress—and there is a need for more light: "Let your light shine before men, that they may see your good works and glorify your Father which is in heaven" (Matthew 5:16).

Secondly, if we let our lights go out, we will miss out on a great opportunity to let others know what the Lord has done for us. You see, the Lord has done great things for us. Yes, He has. He has brought us from a mighty long way. He has brought us out of darkness into His marvelous light. He has opened doors for us that no man can close and closed doors that no man can open.

He's been our help in ages past and He is our hope for years to come. He's been bread when we were hungry and water when we were thirsty. Somebody needs to know that. Somebody needs to know that He's been a bridge over troubled water—a rock in a weary land—a shelter in the time of storm. Some years ago I sang in the choir, and one song that we used to sing I will always remember. It went something like this:

> Since the Savior has turned your sadness
> Into a beautiful life of gladness,
> Keep your light shining, faithful Christian,
> on the way, for Jesus.
>
> Tell life's eternal story,
> As you travel along to glory;
> Keep your light shining, shining, shining,
> Brighter each day.

We need to let the world know that there's not a friend like the lowly Jesus, no, not one. Jesus gave me a little light and told me to let it shine.

A BACCALAUREATE ADDRESS[9]

*"Brethren, I count not myself to have apprehended;
but this one thing I do, forgetting those things which
are behind, and reaching forth unto those things which
are before, I press toward the mark for the prize of the
high calling of God in Christ Jesus" (Philippians 3:13-14).*

To the clergy, administrators, faculty, family and friends, and, most specifically, to the class of '78; how honored I am to be the speaker for this great occasion.

I strongly suspect that along with an overwhelming feeling of jubilation and relief, that there is a strong feeling of accomplishment and satisfaction on the part of the members of this graduating class.

I also suspect that this class of '78 is no different than classes of previous years that were leaving high school for the final time. You're glad it's over and I know you're glad.

I remember how our class of a few years ago reacted during its final days. There was a little chant making the rounds in those final days and we sang it until they were almost ready to throw us out. I hope the teachers will forgive me for bringing it up again. It went like this:

No more classes,
No more books,
No more teacher's dirty looks.

Now, that kind of thing isn't being done today; today's students are a little more refined than we were. We had a glorious time marching through the halls, singing the chanting, and congratulating each other on making it.

And for us that little chant meant that the long, hard struggle was finally over; that the toil and the uphill grind had come to an end and we were free to do as we pleased—to sleep late in the mornings and use our time in whatever manner we saw fit.

However, we soon discovered, to our dismay, that it was not over. That it was, in fact, only the beginning. We soon discovered that there were rougher days ahead and more difficult situations to be faced. Getting out of high school was only the beginning for us.

And, I want to suggest to this graduating class that it isn't over for you either. I say that because, some of your thoughts might possibly be running in a similar vein as did ours. And I would have you to know that what you have accomplished in these few years of study is only the beginning of a longer and more difficult struggle.

You have only reached the first step in the task of achievement. You will soon discover that there are other steps that must be taken. And, if life is to be meaningful and fulfilling, these steps must be given a great deal of consideration, time, energy, and effort.

---

[9]This message was given to the 1978 graduating class of Farrell High School.

The first of these steps is setting goals for yourselves.

Now, some of you have already made your plans and you know what you are going to do. Some of you will go on to college to further prepare yourselves to meet life.

Some will go to vocational school to develop technical skills. Some will go directly into jobs that are even now waiting for them. Others will spend many restless hours looking for employment, which won't be easy—for unemployment is one of the critical problems facing young people in this country.

But, whatever the case, without a specific goal in mind, chances are life will be empty and almost meaningless. In relation to this, Henry Ward Beecher once said, "The successful person is one who marks out for himself the object for which he seeks. He selects a destination and then travels with a distinct purpose toward it."

"No man ever builds accidentally," he continued, "taking here a stone and there a brick, and putting them down with a trowel and mortar by chance, and then looking to see what the sum of all his separate acts amount to."

"It would amount to a confused heap and no building. One selects a place, chooses a plan, and lays the foundation according to a prescribed idea, and then builds tier upon tier definitely and purposefully." Now, that's good sound logic, and I suggest that you consider it carefully in planning your career. Very carefully.

The second of these steps is perseverance. There isn't much value in setting a goal if you fail to give it, not just your best, but more than your best. Goals must be given every ounce of energy that can be mustered, and all of the effort that is possible to put into them.

Perseverance, according to Webster, means *continuing to do something in spite of difficulties and obstacles.* It means steadfastness, stubbornness, and persistence. That's how you must approach whatever task you set out to do. Approach it in a persistent, stubborn manner. Refuse to be side-tracked or put off. Don't let anyone tell you that it can't be done.

Clarence B. McCartney, former minister of the First Presbyterian Church of Pittsburgh, once said, "It is not doing something brilliant or striking that wins you the victory and brings you to the journey's end, but keeping everlastingly at it; sailing on from port to port, island to island, this day and then the next day."

Every once in a while, we sing an old spiritual in our church that dates back to the days of slavery. It was rather crudely written but the message it contains is clear. It says;

"Don't let nobody turn you around,
Keep on to Galilee."

That's what I would say to you today. Don't let anyone or anything pressure you into doing less than the thing that you have set your sights on—nothing or anything.

The third and most notable step: forgetting the past and setting your sights on the present and the future. This is one of the most prolific thoughts that comes out of the passage that was read previously. It was written by the Apostle Paul, a man who was very familiar with the meaning of success and failure, a man who was well versed in terms of knowledge and accomplishments. In it, Paul suggests that the memory of past successes and attainments may prevent us from greater and more splendid accomplishments.

The temptation, he suggests, is to make the past the standard and thus, cut down the possibilities of the present and the future. So he says is, it would be better to forget the past than to look back with a sense of satisfaction.

Now Paul was right. For contentment with the past is fatal to all progress. Therefore, we must forget past attainments in order to forge ahead to bigger and better things. A great philosopher once said, "It is the looking back that endangers the climber who is pressing upward. His one hope in reaching the summit is by forgetting the things behind him and grinding onward."

Now, I don't mean by this that you are to forget what you have learned these past years. I simply mean not to let this accomplishment become a stumbling block to greater accomplishments. Use what you have learned as stepping stones to higher and more rewarding achievements. Let it be the means by which you climb the ladder of success.

Now, even if these steps are followed, the task won't be easy. There will be times in which you will become discouraged and feel like giving up. Therefore, as you persistently strive to reach your goals and ensure for yourself a brighter future, keep in mind the words written by Edward A. Guest:

When things go wrong and they sometimes will,
When the road you're trudging seems all up hill,
When the funds are low and the debts are high,
And you want to smile but you have to sigh,
When cares are pressing you down a bit,
Rest if you must, but don't you quit.

Life is queer with its twists and turns,
As everyone of us sometimes learn,
And many a failure turns about
When he might have won had he stuck it out.
Don't give up though the pace seems slow,
You may succeed with another blow.

Often the goal is nearer than it seems
to a faint and faltering man,
Often the struggler has given up
When he might have captured the victor's cup;
And he learned too late when the night slipped down,
How close he was to the golden crown.

Success is failure turned inside out,
The silver tint of the clouds of doubt;
And you never can tell how close you are
It may be near when it seems afar;

So stick to the fight when you're hardest hit
It's when things seem worst that you mustn't quit.

THE FORMULA FOR SUCCESS

**"Now then he had left speaking, he said unto Simon,
'Launch out in deep, and let down your nets for a draught'" (Luke 5:1-7).**

One day as Jesus was teaching by the shore of Lake Gennesaret, the crowd, in its eagerness to hear His words, almost forced Him into the water. But Jesus noticed two boats standing idly by and entered into one of them owned by a man named Simon, who was later called Peter, and asked him to thrust out a little from the land so that He might teach from the boat.

Simon complied with the request. When Jesus finished teaching, He sought to reward him for his deed. He said, "Launch out into the deep and let down your nets for a draught."

Simon replied, saying, "Master, we have toiled all night and have taken nothing. Nevertheless, at thy word, I will let down my net" (Luke 5:5). When he had done so, he caught a miraculous draught of fish. So many, in fact, that he had to summons help from the other boat to haul them in. His catch was so great that it overloaded both boats and they began to sink.

Whether it was meant to be or not, the command of Jesus to launch out into the deep has become one of the most profound symbols of success ever recorded. It has been acclaimed as the determining factor between success and failure.

The history of our nation and the progress of mankind, in general, are alive with stories of men responsible for great forward movements. They succeeded mainly because they reached out beyond the unknown or launched out into the deep and let down their nets.

There would be no America today if Columbus or someone with similar courage had not launched out. We would be without modern conveniences if someone had not launched out into a far-fetched idea and turned it into a reality. Our astronauts could not have landed on the moon if they had not launched out into the deep of outer space.

Consider with me, if you will, the meaning of the phrase, "Launch out into the deep." It means to explore, venture out, take a chance, or go a little further. It means to trust more in God.

It implies that one must be adventurous if he is to succeed in life. Now adventurous does not mean rushing headlong into a situation, but to make every possible preparation to accomplish every objective and then trusting God for the supply of that which is needed to make the effort a success. A man does not build a tower, said Jesus, without first sitting down and counting the cost.

There are many instances in which individuals and nations have failed to capitalize on ideas or opportunities because they were afraid to launch out into the deep. This is also true as it relates to our religious experiences.

Many churches and church-related programs are suffering because of the lack of spiritual, physical, and financial support. The Christian movement is almost at a standstill because Christians are unable to advance beyond a certain point in their relationship with other Christians. Spiritual visions are blurred and insights have become darkened, all because Christians are content to live close to the shore—live in what is considered to be spiritual safety or spiritual comfort, accepting all spiritual profits—gifts that God blesses all men with.

It's a shame to say it, but men have formed a shallow opinion about God as it relates to His ability to bless us to accomplish certain objectives. As a result, they keep Him bottled up within the walls of the church building. He's almighty God in prayer meetings. He is the ruler of the universe when men are siting in the pews on Sunday mornings, but in business meetings and on the job on Monday, He is of no value.

Man's shallow view of God affects his physical progress as well as his spiritual. A lot of good opportunities have gone down the drain because men were afraid of launching out in faith.

By way of example, a preacher friend of mine in upstate New York told me a story a few years ago of how he tried unsuccessfully to organize a group of citizens in his community to purchase a whole city block that was up for sale (in the middle of town). Acquiring this property would have tremendously improved the economic and social standard of the people of that area. It would have given the small business people of the community an opportunity to move out of the old, broken down, shabby-looking, rat-infested stores they operated and move into decent comfortable surroundings.

He presented them with the plan and everyone agreed that it was a good one and that the project was worthy of investing in, but the deal fell through. The night they were to meet to consummate it, thirty-eight of the forty people contacted failed to come up with the requirements because they were afraid of the possibility of losing their investment. They were afraid to launch out—afraid to take a chance.

So many people are like that. If you don't offer an instant return on their investment, you can forget it. If you don't show them where they can double their money within a week, forget it.

The same thought can be applied to some people's religious aspirations. They expect instant return on their religious investments. If God doesn't bless them the minute they profess religion, if He doesn't kill all their enemies and give them all of their heart's desires right then, you can forget it. They go back into the world with the attitude, "I knew there wasn't anything to it to begin with."

In every venture or undertaking in which we become involved, whether it is large or small, spiritual or physical, there looms the constant danger of disappointment or failure. But, if success is to be achieved, one must be ready to launch out into the deep.

Peter made three discoveries that morning when he obeyed Christ's command. He discovered, first, that the formula for success lies in the difference between fishing in shallow waters and deep waters. Listen again to what happened. When Peter let down his net, he caught a miraculous draught of fish, so many that his net began to break and he had to call for help from the shore. This could not have happened if he had not obeyed the command to launch out into the deep. It is impossible to fill a net while fishing in shallow waters. You might be successful in landing a few minnows, but they are barely enough to whet the appetite.

One of the tragedies of today is that men are content to live in the shallow waters of life rather than venturing out into the deep where true happiness lies. They are content to live on the bare necessities of life, on just enough to get by, on just enough to keep body and soul together. This is tragic to paddle like little children on the beach when the greater prize is in the deep.

The second discovery Peter made was that success is not always attributed to knowledge, nor failure to the lack of it. It lies in the spirit or the attitude of the individual. A man's outlook on life has a lot to do with whether he succeeds or fails. If his outlook is good, he stands a good chance of succeeding, but, if his outlook is bad, he is destined for failure.

Peter's attitude was not the best in the world, but he listened and he obeyed. Let's not forget, he knew what he was doing. He knew the fishing business. This is how they earned their livelihood. They knew the lake on which they were fishing for they had fished there a long time. They knew their boats. In short, they were considered experts in the fishing field.

But listen again to Peter's reply to Christ's command to launch out into the deep: "Master, we have toiled all night and have taken nothing. Nevertheless, at thy word, I will let down the net."

This was a mild protest but, if it had been modern-day Peter, or, Peter with a bad attitude, the reply would have been boisterous. Something to this effect, "Man, there ain't no fish in there. I know these waters. I've been fishing here all my life and I know it ain't nothing down there. And anyway, I'm tired. I've been out here all night. I'm going home to get some rest." This kind of attitude is characteristic of a lot of people today.

Notice the contrasting features of the reward of the modem-day Peter as opposed to the Peter of the text. The modern-day Peter spends his life fishing in shallow waters and catching little or nothing, while the Peter of the text loads his boat to capacity with an abundance of good things.

The third discovery Peter made was that if Jesus is in the boat, success is guaranteed. With Jesus in the boat, he would have no reason to doubt and no reason to fear. And that's all I want to leave with you today, my friends. We can make it in life and we will be successful in all our endeavors if we keep Jesus in our boats. We don't have to fear the unknown if we have Jesus in our boats, for Jesus is the God of the unknown. If His directions are followed, there is no need to fear. If His will be done, the objectives are a certainty.

Listen, the formula is still the same today. It is following our Lord's directions. It is launching out into the deep. It is trusting the Lord. It is stretching out on him. Malachi 3:10 says, "Prove me (or try me) and see if I will not open the windows of heaven and pour you out a blessing that there shall not be room enough to receive it."

If we try Him, if we stretch out on Him, life will be sweeter. Like will be more profitable. It will be more rewarding. As it is written, says Paul, "Eye hath not seen, nor ear heard, neither has it entered into the heart of man the things which God has prepared for them that love him" (1 Corinthians 2:9).

There is no failure in God!

SECTION FOUR
REVEREND DOCTOR RICHARD W. WINGFIELD

Pastor Richard W. Wingfield is a native of western Pennsylvania. A third-generation pastor paternally and a fourth generation pastor maternally, he has more than thirty years in the gospel ministry and serves as the visionary and senior pastor of the Unity Baptist Church of Braddock, Pennsylvania.

Licensed and ordained to the gospel ministry from the Sunset Baptist Church, Grand Prairie, Texas, Pastor Wingfield received his public education from the Farrell Area School District, Farrell, PA. Upon his call to the ministry, he attended the Southern Bible Institute of Dallas, Texas. He received the Associate of Arts degree from Geneva College at the Center for Urban Biblical Ministry where he has the distinction of being the first official graduate. He received the Bachelor of Science degree in community ministry from Geneva College, Beaver Falls, PA. He is a graduate of Pittsburgh Theological Seminary with the Master of Divinity degree and the Doctor of Ministry degree with a focus in pastoral theology.

Pastor Wingfield has extensive pastoral experience having previously served as pastor of the Greater St. Mark Baptist Church of Wichita Falls, Texas; the St. Paul Baptist Church of Donora, PA.; and the Bethel Baptist Church of Braddock, PA.

Among his varied involvements, Pastor Wingfield serves as a member of the board of directors as well as a faculty member of the Center for Urban Biblical Ministry. He also serves as an adjunct faculty member for the Adult Degree Completion Program for Geneva College. He has served as the Theological Enrichment Chairperson for the Baptist Minister's Conference of Pittsburgh and Vicinity, an instructor for the Certificate of Progress Program (COPP School) for the Allegheny Union Baptist Association Congress of Christian Education, president of the Greater Braddock Ministerial Association, a member of the Citizen's Council for Gateway Braddock, and a member of the advisory board for the Metro Urban Institute of Pittsburgh Theological Seminary. Along with his varied activities, Pastor Wingfield now serves as moderator of the Allegheny Union Baptist Association of western Pennsylvania.

Pastor Wingfield has a passion for the education for those in the ministry and serves as a mentor to a number of pastors and ministers across the Pittsburgh area. Pastor Wingfield's personal desire is to "... to know Christ and the power of his resurrection and the fellowship of his sufferings being conformed to his death."

Pastor Wingfield is married to the love of his life, best friend and confidant, the former Vanessa Clifton, and they are the proud parents of three adult children and three grandchildren.

THE CONTEXT

Rev. Wingfield preaches during a time when the present generation is an unchurched generation. He seeks to be relevant in preaching, addressing the social issues of the day and how the gospel of Jesus Christ relates to what is transpiring around the world.

The age is also an age of technology where people are multi-tasking people. He is not as poetic as his predecessors, though he has been known to use the idiom of the day.

He is theologically a moderate and ascribes more fully to liberation theology. He is basically a flat-footed preacher, though he too will leave the pulpit for the purposes of emphasis. He has a traditional style of Black preaching with contemporary imagery.

BREAKING THROUGH THE BARRIERS

**"And we were in our own sight was grasshoppers,
and so we were in their sight" (Numbers 13:26-33).**

Have you ever experienced the feeling that no matter how hard you try, you could not make it? Have you ever felt like giving up even before you get started because things seem so bleak and impossible? Have you ever felt that the best you could do would not be good enough—that no matter what you would do you it would still fall short of your intended goal?

Rest assured that you are not the only one who has experienced these feelings. For all of us have had:

- mountains that seemed insurmountable,
- roads that seemed impassable,
- hills that seemed invincible, and
- things that seemed unconquerable.

This is how many view new horizons in their lives—with a sense of apprehension, fearing what is around the corner, apprehensive about what may transpire during the coming year, days, and moments. No, you do not know what tomorrow may hold. One moment you can be up and the next moment you can be down. One moment, you can be the picture of health and the next moment sickness can invade your body. One moment, there can be joy and ecstasy and the next moment there can be sorrow and sadness. Life is just that unpredictable.

Nevertheless, each day brings to us new challenges and a sense of hope. A new day in our lives symbolically speaks of a new lease on life. It gives us another opportunity to:

- right some wrongs,
- make amends for some erroneous judgments, and
- alter some bad decisions we have made.

And we might as well come to grips with the fact that all of us, at some point in our lives, have made some mistakes. I don't care how long you have been on the glory road, all of us have made some bad decisions and some errors in our judgments. And because of these shortcomings, we face life with apprehensive anticipation—not knowing what is around the corner but thankful to God that we have one more chance.

Because of this shortcoming, we resolve within ourselves that the next time: "I'm going to do better." "I'm not going to do this, but that instead." "I'll do that rather than doing this."

And many of the things we resolve to do are broken the very same day because even though we have the desire, something hinders us from accomplishing our goal. And I have discovered that most of the time it is not an outside influence but something on the inside that prevents us from reaching our goal.

That's why we fall short. That's why we have such a hard time pulling it all together. The desire is there. Deep down within, we really want to accomplish our goal. We're at the brink of:

- kicking that habit,
- licking that problem,
- nipping that situation in the bud.

But something within, at the very last moment, always causes us to stumble and fall.

Have you ever felt that way? It's within your reach, it's within your grasp, but you just can't seem to grab hold of your victory. Something on the inside of you:

- hinders you,
- stifles you,
- tells you that you can't do it,
- holds you back, and your victory manages to stay out of your reach time and time again.

And whenever you face failure after failure, frustration sets in. You begin to get down on yourself and blame yourself because you just can't break this vicious cycle. If you can just catch hold of it:

- everything would be all right,
- you'll accomplish what you set out to do,
- you can move from point A to point B.

Have you ever felt that way? This is where you may be today. God has a host of abundant blessings for us. God wants us to experience the abundance of His grace. God wants us to experience the blessedness of His presence. God wants us to experience the fullness of His Spirit, and many of us are standing in the pathway of blessing. Many of us are standing at the threshold, at the brink of:

- salvation,
- deliverance,
- receiving your miracle,
- receiving your healing,
- having unspeakable joy,
- peace that passes all understanding,
- kicking that unmentionable habit,
- security in your relationship with Christ,

but something within you is causing you to miss the blessing that God has in store for you.

If you're at this point in your life, you are in need of a breakthrough. There are some strong-holds that need to be pulled down in your life. Understand that this is spiritual warfare. The devil is wreaking havoc on the body of Christ and we are allowing the devil to gain victories and win battles that he has no business winning. That's why we need to put on the whole armor of God, for we need to recognize who the enemy really is. "For we wrestle not against flesh and blood. . ." (Ephesians 6:12).

The nation of Israel was at this point. They were at the brink of blessing. For 430 years, they were captives in Egypt, and when they had reached the point of despair, they cried unto the Lord in their trouble and He delivered them from all their distresses. By the power of God and the blood of the Lamb, He delivered them from Egyptian oppression. Look at how God provided for them as they traveled in the wilderness. God:

- provided manna from heaven to feed them,
- sweetened the waters of Meribah when they were thirsty,
- provided room service with roast quail for dinner,
- delivered them from the conflict with Amalek,
- divinely guided them with a pillar of cloud by day and pillar of fire by night.

God had already done great things for Israel. Now Israel was at the brink of entering the Promised Land—the land of Canaan, the land flowing with milk and honey. Canaan is significant in Scripture for it was the place of rest, blessing, and security. In preparation for the conquest of the land, Moses sent out twelve spies, one from each tribe, to survey the land. He gave them specific instructions:

- people—strong or weak; few or many?
- land—good or bad; rich or poor?
- cities—camps or strongholds?
- bring back fruit from the land.

They went out as instructed to spy out the land and after forty days, they returned with their report but there was disagreement among the spies. Ten spies brought back a negative report:

"Yes, the land is flowing with milk and honey. It is a rich land. Yes, the land is all they said it would be and here is some fruit as evidence of the richness of the land. But, what we saw was not good. The people of the land were strong and the cities were fortified. The sons of Anak live there and there is no way that we can defeat the people and possess the land" (Numbers 13:27-29).

But there were two spies, Joshua and Caleb by name, who brought back a positive report, and they felt that Israel should immediately go up and possess the land because, they said, "We are well able" (Numbers 13:30).

Now, what has always intrigued me about this scenario is that all twelve of these spies went out to spy out the land together, they returned to the camp together, they compared notes and came up with the same facts, yet they still ended up with two conflicting conclusions plus a lopsided vote. And I wondered how in the world this could be?

It could have been that there were a couple among the spies who were a little more vocal than the others and were able to persuade them to go along with them. You know what I'm talking about, for in our churches we have some folk who are a little more opinionated than others and through brashness and intimidation are able to control the outcome of things.

But when I looked a little bit further, I discovered that as the spies weighed the facts, Joshua and Caleb added another dimension to the scale. What was that dimension? That dimension was faith, and faith tipped the scale.

(EXPAND) Israel making the motion not to go up and possess the land. Joshua and Caleb: "No, for we are well able for we have faith."

And this leads me to my first point in the analysis. If you want to get out of the rut of disappointment and failure and experience a breakthrough in your life, you need to learn to *see things through the eyes of faith.*

One of the biggest hindrances to receiving the blessings that God has for us is the failure to believe God and His word. We fail to believe that God is able to do what He says He will do.

The ten spies returned with a negative report. Listen to what they said: "There are giants in the land. The sons of Anak are in the land and we are not equipped mentally or physically to deal with these giants"

Israel believed the report of these ten spies and as a result of their faithlessness, an eleven-day trip turned into a forty-year nightmare. They spent forty years:

- wandering in the wilderness,
- going in circles,
- licking their wounds.

The Israelite dilemma is the same dilemma that exists among the people of God: a lack of spiritual vision. We cannot experience breakthroughs in our lives or in the life of the church because we fail to see things through the eyes of faith. When we fail to see things through the eyes of faith, rather than standing on the promises,

- we wind up sifting on the premises,
- we end up wandering in the wilderness of doubt, despondency and despair,
- we tend to see obstacles as bigger than what they really are.

ILLUSTRATION: 2 Kings 8——Elisha and the Syrian army.

APPLICATION: Experiencing a breakthrough means that we have to deal with some giants, those things that seem to be insurmountable, those things that seem undefeatable. But let the giants come. Bring on the giants, for I have found out that the bigger they are, the harder they fall. When we see things through the eyes of faith, we will discover that God rewards our faith. Hebrews 11:6.

And I am convinced that what the church needs are more Joshuas and Calebs who are not afraid to add faith to the equation and who are not afraid to step out on the promises of God, regardless of the facts.

- FACTS: The odds are against us.
     FAITH: With God all things are possible . . .
- FACTS: We can't pull this off.
     FAITH: I can do all things through Christ . . .
- FACTS: We're in the minority.
     FAITH: If God be for us . . .
- FACTS: We're the underdogs.
     FAITH: We're more than conquerors . . .
- FACTS: We're going to lose.
     FAITH: Thanks be to God who gives us the victory.

We must learn to see things through the eyes of faith.

Second, if we want to break through the barriers that hinder us, we must learn to *focus on the goal and not on the people.*

Joshua and Caleb were in the minority. Yet, even though they were in the minority, even though they were ridiculed, even though they were almost stoned, they did not concern themselves with the majority report. They were men of principle and stood for what they believed.

I don't know why it is, but there are some folk who don't want to see anyone succeed. There are some folk in this world who don't want anyone to get ahead. There are some folk who are hell-bent on destroying your spirit, defaming your name, and decapitating your reputation. There are some folk who are always trying to bring you down and keep you down.

ILLUSTRATION: The proverbial barrel of crabs

Listen to what they say, "They ain't nothing and will never amount to anything. They ain't going nowhere and ain't going to do nothing. I remember them when . . ."

We must learn to focus on the goal and not people. Because Joshua and Caleb focused on the goal, because they did not allow the majority to sway them, Joshua and Caleb were the only two of that generation of Israelites to enter the Promised Land. Listen to the request of Caleb forty-five years later in Joshua 14:

> "I was forty years old when Moses sent me out to spy out the land. And because I wholly followed the Lord, Moses swore to me that the land upon which I set my foot was to be mine inheritance. The Lord has kept me alive these forty-five years, and I am not ready for the rocking chair. I am as strong now was I was then. Now, therefore, give me this mountain . . ., and if the Lord be with me, I will drive out the enemy."

If you're bogged down with trying to please people, I have a word for you today. Don't ever let anybody dictate to you what you can and cannot do. Don't ever let anyone dictate to you what you can and cannot be. For there is always someone who is trying to keep you at a level where they can control you. Don't let no one stop you from receiving what God has in store for you. *Don't let nobody turn you around!*

Finally, if you want to experience a spiritual breakthrough in your life, *don't dwell on what you don't have, but concentrate on what you do have.*

You see, the problem with these ten spies was that they wanted to analyze their own situation. Israel was at the doorstep of the Promised Land and all they had to do was to go over and possess the land. But because they looked at the situation rather than looking at God, they developed a grasshopper mentality. They said, "We are as grasshoppers in their sight and our own sight" (Numbers 13:33).

Look at it. Nobody told them they were grasshoppers. That was their own assessment of their situation. That was their own perception of their predicament.

Too many times, we are guilty of trying to analyze our own situations, and by analyzing our situations we limit our ability to perform. When we analyze our situation, we will always end up with the short end of the stick. Listen to what we say, "Because I don't have this talent or that skill, what I have doesn't really amount to much. What I have really doesn't make a difference or an impact."

As a result, we live below the means that God has intended for us. Why? Because we dwell so much on what we don't have to the neglect of what we do have.

"Well, you just don't jump into things. You've got to develop a focus group/task force. You've got to do a case study. You've got to analyze this thing."

Analyze this! It doesn't take much for God to accomplish his mission:

- David only had a slingshot and five smooth stones, but, with God, he had dead aim.
- Moses only had a rod in his hand, but, with God, he told Pharaoh, "Let my people go . . ."
- Gideon only went to battle with 300 men, but, with God, they defeated the Midianite army.
- Samson only had the jawbone of an ass, but with God, he subdued the Philistines.
- Jesus only had a borrowed lunch of two fish and five loaves of bread, but He prepared a banquet in the desert.

My point is this:

- We may not have houses and land, but we serve a God who holds the wealth of the world in his hand.
- We may not have wealth and financial security, but we serve a God who is able to supply our every need.
- We may not be able to sing like angels, but we serve a God who gives songs in the night.
- We may not be able to preach like Paul, but we serve a God who gives us a testimony.
- We may not be able to understand the dark clouds of despair, but we serve a God who can roll the dark clouds away.
- We may not be able to understand the storms of life, but we serve a God who can speak peace in the midst of our storms,
- We may not be able to understand why we have to shed briny tears, but we serve a God who can wipe the tears from our eyes,
- We may not know what tomorrow may hold, but we serve a God who knows what is around every corner.
- We may not be able to see our way clearly, but we serve a God who is able to bring us safely through. "Yea, though I walk through the valley . . ."

Conclusion: Chuck Yeager breaking the sound barrier. As he was approaching the sound barrier, the plane began to rattle and shake. People said he wouldn't make it, but he kept on pressing his way until finally he broke the sound barrier and it was smooth sailing from that point on.

The road might get rough, the going might get tough and the hills hard to climb. But if you just hold on, if you keep pressing your way, there is a blessing on the other side of through (rest, peace, unspeakable joy).

"Weeping may endure for a night, but joy comes in the morning" (Psalm 30:5).

I'm going to hold on.

SING YOUR SONG

"How can we sing the Lord's song in a strange land?" (Psalm 137:14).

These words of Psalm 137 are the words of an oppressed people, a people who were beaten, battered, bruised and in bondage under the nation of Babylon. These are the words of a people who were thousands of miles away from home. They were hurting, heavy-laden, and in a seemingly hopeless condition.

For seventy years, they faced suppression, oppression, and repression. For seventy years, they were in a miserable condition. For seventy years, they sat thinking of all the good times they had back home. So miserable were they over their plight that when the captors made a request for them to sing, these people were so downtrodden, dejected, depressed, and demoralized that they could not sing. For whenever they thought of Zion, whenever they thought of the place of worship and communion with God, their longing for it was so great that they just could not hold back the tears.

But, not only could they not sing, but, they would not sing. The captors put in a request for one of Israel's top ten songs, yet, this request was not honored. They hung their harps on the willows of Babylon, not seeking to hide their harps but hanging them in plain view. In other words, the people of God went on strike. And a perennial, provocative, and penetrating reply was given to this request: "How can we sing the Lord's song in a strange land?"

What a sad commentary. The people of God going on strike and refusing to sing. That is a strange response coming from a people of God. That is a strange response coming from a people of whom the Lord declared, "I will be your God and you will be my people" (Exodus 6:7). That is a strange response from a people who were the apple of God's eye. And the question has been raised, "Why would they not sing?"

Dr. David Shannon once suggested that their reasoning for not singing could have been psychological. Being in captivity, being in bondage does not a suggest a good atmosphere in which to sing. Or, he said, their reasoning could have been musical. Their harps could have been hung up in retirement and had to be tuned. However, Dr. Shannon suggests that their reasoning was neither psychological or musical, but it was theological. They did not sing the Lord's song in a strange land because they believed it to be sacrilegious. It was not apropos. This was not the appropriate time to be singing the Lord's song.

And there are many who carry with them this similar mindset. There are many who feel that to sing the Lord's song in the midst of tears and tragedy is disrespectful to the God they serve. There are those who feel that being in the midst of trials and tribulations, oppression and repression, is not a conducive climate for caroling one of the Lord's songs. There are those who believe that singing the Lord's song in the midst of a trying situation is the most ridiculous thing that one can do.

But, I want to suggest to you that it is not. In fact, when you are down and out, when you are oppressed and depressed, when you are perplexed and puzzled, when you are down so low until down begins to look down on you, that's the time to start singing!

Look at our heritage as African-Americans and you will discover that even though our forefathers were in a strange land, even though they were disenfranchised as a people, even though our mothers were raped, even though our fathers were lynched, even though their children grew up fatherless, even though the family was broken up by slave trade; the more the Massa' tried to tear us down, the more Mama sang.

There is a message in this for all of us. No matter how long the day, no matter how dark and difficult the night, no matter how bleak and mitigating the circumstances, don't let nobody take away your song. They may:

- lie on you,
- cheat you,
- talk about you,
- mistreat you,
- criticize you,
- ridicule you,
- call you everything but a child of God, but

don't let anybody stop you from singing your song. "Release your song," saith the Spirit.

I am totally convinced that the Lord's song can be sung in a strange land. You see, the strange land to Israel was Babylon. And in Scripture, Babylon is symbolic of the world system. And, as Israel was in a strange land, we, too, are in a strange land. Grandma put it like this;

"This world is not my home,
I'm a pilgrim traveling through a barren land."

You don't need a college education to realize that a strange land does not hold much hope for us. There are:

- sorrows in this strange land,
- burdens in this strange land,
- heartaches in this strange land,
- heartbreaks in this strange land,
- disappointments in this strange land,
- discouragements in this strange land.

A strange land offers no sanctuary, no security, no solace or no serenity for the people of God. This is a strange land.

Yet, in spite of all that is against us, we ought to be able to sing the Lord's song. We can still sing because praising God is never out of season. Every time we have the opportunity, we should, "Enter into his gates with thanksgiving and into his courts with praise" (Psalm 100:1). For the Bible says,

- "Let the redeemed of the Lord, say so" (Psalm 107:2).
- "Let the high praises of God be in your mouth" (Psalm 149:6).
- "Let everything that hath breath praise the Lord" (Psalm 150:6)
- "Make a joyful noise unto the Lord" (Psalm 98:4).
- "Worthy is the Lamb that was slain" (Revelation 5:12).
- "While I yet live will I praise the Lord" (Psalm 146:2).
- "From the rising of the sun until the going down of the same the Lord is worthy to

be praised" (Psalm 113:3).

Praising God is never out of season!

ILLUSTRATION: You remember Paul and Silas were in jail. And at midnight, they held a prayer service.

APPLICATION: Praising God is never out of season. So why don't you open your mouth and praise the Lord?

We can sing the Lord's song in a strange land. We can sing in a strange land because:

A. We have faith in Almighty God.

Hebrews 11:1 says, "Now faith is the substance of things hope for, the evidence of things not seen." The New English Bible puts it like this: "Faith gives substance to our hopes, and makes us certain of realities we do not see."

Faith is the confident assurance that something we want is going to happen, and is the certainty that what we hope for is waiting for us, even though we cannot see it up ahead. Whatever else you may want to call it, faith is the confidence that God can do anything but fail. It is the confidence that God can make a way out of no way. It is the confidence that God can make the rough places plain and the crooked places straight. It is the confidence that God can handle any situation.

I have discovered that many are unable to sing because they have not allowed their faith to master their circumstances.

ILLUSTRATION: Peter and the disciples on the boat.

This is how many of us react. When trouble comes we press the panic button. When trials come, no longer do we lift up our eyes unto the hills from whence cometh our help, but we lift up our eyes unto the medicine cabinets from whence cometh our tranquilizers. When tribulation comes, we retreat into seclusion, worrying and wondering how am I ever going to get out of this mess!

But when we have faith, regardless of what the circumstances may be, we can still sing one of the Lord's songs. For God can take your mess and give you a message. God can take your test and give you a testimony. We know this because faith exceeds our circumstances. I may not know what tomorrow may hold, but I know who holds tomorrow and I know who holds my hand.

I don't have to give up in despair. I don't have to throw in the towel. I don't have to quit because I have faith that God is able to do exceedingly, abundantly above whatever I should ask or think. I have faith that God is able to:

- wipe tears from my eyes,
- lift my burdens,
- carry my load,
- when in trouble, deliverance surely will come,
- when in danger, He will give me victory,
- when in difficulty, He will make a way somehow.

And if you have the faith, God's got the power and your soul can look back and wonder how you got over!

B. There are those who need to hear us singing.

Whether you realize it or not, your singing can minister to someone's soul. Your singing can soothe a weary soul, quiet a troubled heart, and ease a disturbed spirit. Why? Because there is a message in the music, there is a testimony in the tune, there is a letter in the lyrics.

You see, in the days of slavery, singing was used as a form of communication. When the old slave wanted to call a meeting, he would sing songs like,

"Steal away to Jesus,
I ain't got long to stay here."

When someone failed to show up for the meeting, they would sing,

"I couldn't hear nobody pray."

To spread some bad news, they would sing,

"Over my head, I see trouble in the air."

To spread good news, they would sing,

"Over my head, I hear music in the air."

Well, we sing today to communicate a message to a dying world. For in the midst of turmoil, difficulties, disappointments, and frustrations, the world needs to hear one of the songs of Zion. It needs to hear the gospel message through melody. For in the music there can be found words of salvation, deliverance, comfort, consolation, hope, and rejoicing.

ILLUSTRATION: I remember hearing the congregation singing on our way to church at a time when our forefathers sang out of the depths of their souls. It would do something to you that your walk would turn into a trot and the trot would turn into a run just to get to the sanctuary. You just wanted to be where the action was.

APPLICATION: We must not hang up our harps. We need to sing. Not so much because we love to sing or we have a good voice, but because there are those who need to hear us singing. People are hurting, people are hopeless, people are helpless, and they need to hear a message of hope. Our singing demonstrates that all is not lost. Our singing shows the world that there is still hope on the horizon. Our singing relates that there is a light at the end of the tunnel.

Somebody needs to hear us singing: "There is a balm in Gilead, to make the wounded whole; There is a balm in Gilead, to heal the sin-sick soul." Somebody needs to hear us singing, "Father, I stretch my hands to thee, no other help I know." Somebody needs to hear us singing, "I'm so glad trouble don't last always." Somebody needs to hear us singing, "I love the Lord, He heard my cry, and pitied every groan." Somebody needs to hear us singing, "He knows just how much we can bear." Somebody needs to hear us singing!

C. Something on the inside keeps me singing.

ILLUSTRATION: I was watching television with my son and we were watching a kid's show called *Fraggle Rock*. In this one particular episode, everybody had a song but this one particular fraggle. He wanted a song just like everybody else. Yet, his song would not come forth. Before long, he realized that his song was inside of him and all he had to do was to let it come out.

APPLICATION: I thought about that and I discovered that if you have been born again, you have a song to sing. God has picked you up out of the muck and mire of sin and gave you a new lease on life, you have a song to sing. And every now and then, the fire starts to burn. Every now and then, the prayer wheel begins to turn and you just can't hold your peace. It's just like fire shut up in your bones.

The poet put it like this:

> It's in my heart, this melody of love divine,
> It's in my heart, since I am his and he is mine;
> It's in my heart, how can I help but sing and shine,
> It's in my heart!

I don't know what your song may be. It may be:

- Glory, glory hallelujah
- Amazing grace;
- This little light of mine;
- Guide me, O Thou great Jehovah;
- The Lord will make a way somehow.

But, whatever it may be, you need to sing your song. For the song that you have, the world didn't give it to you and the world can't take it away.

I am sure that you have had the experience of the poet. You were walking around the house with a song on your heart. The thought came, then some humming. Then, before you knew it, you were singing aloud to the glory of God. You may not have been able to carry a tune. You may not have kept the proper tempo. But, in your own way, you were just singing and praising God. You were able to do it because there was:

> "Something within me that holdeth the reins,
> Something within me that banishes pain;
> Something within me I cannot explain,
> All that I know there is something within!"

What is it on the inside? It is the blessedness in knowing that there is someone within, he blessed Holy Spirit, moving on the altars of our hearts who gives songs in the night.

> "When! think of the goodness of Jesus,
> And all He's done for me;
> My soul cries out, 'Hallelujah,
> I thank God for saving me!'"

YOU'RE NEXT IN LINE FOR A MIRACLE

**"When all the jars were full, she said to her son, 'Bring me another one.'
But he replied, 'There is not a jar left.' Then the oil stopped flowing" (2 Kings 4:1-7 NIV).**

It never ceases to amaze me how God can take nothing and make something out of it. It never ceases to amaze me how God can bring great gain out of apparent nothingness.

God demonstrated this at creation. The Bible declares that "the earth was without form and void, and darkness was upon the face of the deep" (Genesis 1:2). But God looked into nothing, stepped onto nothing, spoke into nothing, and the world, by the power of the word of God, came into existence. It never ceases to amaze me how God can take nothing and make something out of it.

God demonstrated this with the creation of man. Man was only a concept in the mind of God, but on the sixth day, God said, "Let us make man in our image, after our likeness" (Genesis 1:26). Then God stooped down, picked up some dirt and began to mold, shape, and configure man according to His specifications and desire. But even after being molded and shaped, man was only a something. He did not become a somebody until God breathed into him the breath of life; then man became somebody, a living soul.

It never ceases to amaze me how God can bring something out of utter nothingness, but that is the way that He works. God is able to take your less than enough and multiply it to more than enough. God can take a seemingly hopeless situation and bring forth great blessings.

We have all experienced hopeless situations. All of us have found ourselves in the midst of some painfully progressive predicaments. We have had our private hells, but isn't it good to know that in the midst of these painfully progressive predicaments, God is able to:

- calm the calamity,
- still the storm,
- heal the heartache, and
- override every obstacle.

Many of us have been down to our last dime and the Lord has made a way. Many of us have been to our "wit's end" wondering what our next move would be, but God made a way out of no way. Many of us have faced stumbling blocks along the road but God showed that he was able to turn those stumbling blocks into stepping stones. That's the way that God works.

Now all that God does is good, but I am convinced beyond the shadow of a doubt that God does His best work when:

- all the chips are down,
- we have come to the end of our rope,
- when all hope seems lost.

For God can bring:

- hope where there is no hope,

- joy in the midst of life's jolts,
- laughter in the midst of lament,
- cheerfulness in the midst of chaos,
- optimism in the midst of oppression.

God works that way.

I'm reminded of that perennial, paramount question that was posed to Abraham: "Is there anything too hard for the Lord?" (see Jeremiah 32:27). And I have found that the answer to this question is a resounding no. For if God can't fix it, it can't be fixed. If God can't do it, it can't be done.

Do you need a miracle? Do you need God to do something out of the ordinary for you? Do you God to suspend the laws of nature and bring about a great blessing for you? God is able to work a miracle in your life. If you need a miracle, I stopped by to tell you to move to the front of the line, for you are next in line for a miracle.

This thought leads us to this historical narrative. Elisha, that great prophet in Israel, was the protégé, the understudy of the prophet Elijah, the one who requested a double portion of the spirit that was in Elijah, the one who picked up Elijah's mantle and carried on the prophetic ministry. Elisha was carrying on his daily routine at the office. While conducting the business of the day, there came to him a certain woman of the wives of the sons of the prophets with an urgent appeal. She found herself in a painfully progressive predicament having to perform what she did not have the resources to do. This woman was in desperate need of a miracle.

Look at her situation. Her husband had died. We don't know much about him; the obituary is rather small, but there are two significant things that are mentioned about him. For one thing, we see that he loved and feared God. Let me put a pin here and suggest to you that when it comes time for you to cross the chilly Jordan, when it comes time for you to lay down your hymnbook and Bible and study war no more, if nothing else can be said about you, you ought to have the witness that you loved and feared God. You ought to have the testimony that you walked with the Lord. When the preacher stands over you and commits your body to the ground, people ought to be able to say that you had a relationship with the Lord Jesus for yourself.

The second thing that we find about this man was that he died in debt. Now we do not know how the debt was incurred. It may be that his illness was a lengthy one and that the medical bills became insurmountable. It may have been that in the midst of seeking to liquidate a current indebtedness, he died suddenly leaving the accounts unpaid.

We don't know how he ended up in debt, but we do know that he died owing a great sum of money. The insurance policy was apparently barely enough to cover the burial expenses and his widow was left, not only to grieve the death of her friend, lover, husband, and man, but to also deal with a debt that she could not pay. The credit agency became weary of the delay in payment and no further arrangements could be made. The creditors were merciless. They were not concerned over the recent loss of her husband. They were not concerned about the fact that she had two young boys to raise all by herself. The only thing they were concerned about was that the debt had to be paid. And since, according to the Jewish law, her sons were considered as assets, the creditors were ready to take her sons as collateral to pay off the debt.

This woman was in a painfully progressive predicament. She had come to the end of her rope. All of her resources were exhausted and all hope was apparently gone. Distressed, desperate, destitute, and in debt, she held on to one last glimmer of hope. She remembered that God was:

- the God of the oppressed,
- a Father to the fatherless,
- the judge of the widow,

So she went not to the psychic hot line, but she went to the man of God to seek counsel of the Lord.

Where do you go when the winds of adversity blow? Where do you go when the walls begin to cave in on you? Where do you go when the clouds of disillusionment, discouragement, and despair cover your sky? I stopped by to tell you that when you are in distress, if you need a shelter, if you need a friend, you better be sure that your anchor holds and grips that solid rock.

The psalmist said, "When my soul is overwhelmed; lead me to the rock that is higher than I" (Psalm 61:2). The psalmist said, "He only is my rock and my salvation; he is my defense" (Psalm 62:6).

She went to Elisha, the man of God, but understand that her trust was not in the prophet, but in the God of the prophet. She knew Elisha to be God's ambassador. Therefore, she was able to submit herself to and comply with God's Word through His prophet.

Elisha asked her, "How can I help you? What do you have in your house?" And after conversation with her, he found out that all she had was a cruse, a small bowl of oil. Elisha said to her, "Woman, that's all God needs. For just a little bit in God's hand goes a long way."

You see, it is the little things that God is pleased to use. It doesn't take God much to accomplish what needs to get done. God's help starts from what we already have. And if we are to experience a miracle, there must be a willingness to turn it over to Him to be used to His disposal. What do you have in your house that you can turn over to Him? That's the question for you to consider today. What do you have in your house that God can take control of? What do you have in your house that can be put to God's disposal? Whatever you have for His disposal, learn to put it all in the hands of God. In your hands, it's not much, but in God's hands, it can be used to bring about abundant blessing.

Elisha gave this unnamed woman some specific instructions. He told the woman, "Go and borrow some vessels from your neighbors. Go everywhere you can and borrow as many as you can. And when you have come in, shut the door. This miracle is just for you and your sons." If you want to experience God's greatest blessings, you have to shut the world out, and shut God in. And if you do it God's way, He has a special blessing just for you. He's got a blessing with your name on it. God wants to minister specifically to you. The more I look at it, the more I believe that there are some blessings God has in store for us that are not intended to be publicized.

Observe that she did exactly what the prophet said. According to his word, she acted. She went and borrowed not two or three vessels, but many vessels, as many as she could possibly find. This is significant because there is a recurrent theme throughout the Bible that stands as a test of whether or not we want to receive God's blessings, i.e. faith and obedience. Both of these go hand in hand. The one cannot be divorced from the other.

Hebrews 11:1 and 6 says faith is believing God. It is the confidence that God will do what He says He will do. Faith is taking God at His word. If faith is believing in God's word, obedience is acting upon God's word. It is doing exactly what God has instructed us to do. They both go hand in hand. One cannot do without the other. And many of us miss God's greatest blessings for us simply because we do not act upon faith by obedience. Faith says, "I may not be able to see it right now, but if God said it, I am going to step out on God's word."

The underlying principle is that obedience brings blessings. And let me remind you of something: Don't always look for material blessings. I know that God is able to give you the money you need. I know that He is able to give you what you need to pay your bills, but God's blessings stretch beyond the material. For He also blesses us, as the old prayer warriors used to say, with a reasonable portion of health and strength. The blood still running warm in our veins and clothed in our right minds. That's a blessing. The fact that He saved us when we were a wretch undone. That's a blessing. The fact that He picked us up out of the muck and mire of sin and placed us on a solid rock, that's a blessing. In fact, we don't have to wait until the battle is over, we can have a shout out right now. For when I think of the goodness of Jesus, and all He's done for me . . .

Notice that according to the number of vessels she borrowed, so was her faith. The text shows us that as long as she had empty vessels, the oil kept pouring, but as soon as she ran out of vessels, the oil stopped. My point is that too many times, because of our lack of faith, we limit God's blessings for us. We stay God's hand upon us when we really don't trust God. God's blessings are multiple. He is able to do exceedingly and abundantly above all that we should ask or think.

- He is able to bless us beyond measure.
- He is able to give unto us good measure, pressed down, shaken together, and running over.
- He is able to open the windows of heaven and pour out a blessing.

If this woman had only gathered a few vessels, she might not have had enough money to pay her debts, but because she took God at His word, she was able to get out of debt and live comfortably on the rest. God took her less than enough and provided more than enough.

You might not have much, but little becomes much when you place it in the Master's hand. For God has a way of

- turning predicaments into potential,
- taking hopeless situations and bringing great hope,
- turning a burdensome circumstance into great and abundant blessing,
- turning your mess into a message,
- turning your test into a testimony.

When God blesses you, you have a testimony. Let me call up some witness and let them Testify:

- David said, "I've been young, and now I'm old. But I've never seen the righteous forsaken, nor his seed begging bread" (Psalm 37:25).
- Job declares, "All the days of my appointed time will I wait until my change comes" (Job 14:14).
- Isaiah says, "They that wait upon the Lord shall renew their strength" (Isaiah 40:31).
- David said, "The mercy of the Lord is from everlasting to everlasting upon those who fear him and his righteousness unto his children's children" (Psalm 103:17).
- The psalmist said, "No good thing will he withhold from them that walks uprightly" (Psalm 84:11).

- James said, "Every good and perfect gift comes from the Father" (James 1:17).
- Paul said, "My God shall supply all your need" (Philippians 4:19).

Do you need a miracle in your life? Do you need God to do something for you right now? I'm a witness that He is able to make a way somehow. So get ready, for you are next in line for a miracle. This is your day for a miracle. This is your day for a breakthrough. This is your day for deliverance. No matter what the devil may say, move to the front of the line, for you are next in line for a miracle. It's yours for the asking.

"God specializes in things that are impossible;
and He can do what no other power can do!"

TOO LEGIT TO QUIT

**"So I sent messengers to them with this reply,
'I am carrying on a great project
and cannot go down. Why should the work stop
while I leave it and go down to you?'" (Nehemiah 6:3).**

Music has always been an integral part of the African American experience. Each decade has brought new artists, a new sound, and a new means of expression. From

- Cab Calloway to Smokey Robinson to Luther Vandross,
- Billie Holliday to Aretha Franklin to Whitney Houston,
- Platters to Earth, Wind and Fire to NWA,

African American music has served as a means of expression to raise the consciousness of our people and to help us run this race a little while longer.

A few years ago, Hammer came out with a rap entitled, *Too Legit to Quit.* In it he speaks of a determination to make it in spite of the opposition that may come and the odds that are stacked against him. Now, I am not a rapper, I cannot rap and I am not going to try to rap. But I would like to suggest to you that if Nehemiah were living today, I believe he would have adopted these words as his motto. For his life demonstrated in word and in deed one that was committed to the task. I want to suggest to you that Nehemiah was "too legit to quit."

The story of Nehemiah is an interesting story filled with many messages that are relevant to our society and our mission. You will recall that Nehemiah was the cupbearer—the wine taster for King Artaxerxes who was the king of the Persian empire. This was a position of honor and importance, and Nehemiah performed his duties well. Yet, his desire and concern was for the welfare of his people back in the land of his fathers, Jerusalem.

Upon the arrival of brethren from Judah, Nehemiah asked them concerning the welfare of those who had survived the captivity and about his hometown of Jerusalem. The report that he received, however, was not favorable. The walls of the city were broken down, the gates were burned with fire, and the people were distressed and discouraged.

The record declares that when Nehemiah heard these things, immediately he went down in prayer and asked God for favor before the king. And Scripture verifies that if you pray and pray right, God will answer your prayer. God answered Nehemiah's prayer. For while Nehemiah was performing his daily duties before the king, Artaxerxes noticed that Nehemiah was not his old self. He could tell that something was wrong with Nehemiah. You can always tell when someone's mind is preoccupied. The king asked Nehemiah what was on his mind. Nehemiah explained the situation and was granted permission from the king to return to his homeland and receive the necessary supplies to rebuild the walls of the city.

So Nehemiah returned to Jerusalem, scoped out the situation, and began the building project. And don't you know, even in the midst of a good situation, Satan always manages to throw a monkey wrench in the plan. Nehemiah faced opposition from two sources. For one, there were those from the outside that did not approve of the building project. Sanballat, Tobiah, and others ridiculed the building program. So bad was the ridicule that Tobiah said, "Even if a fox climbed the wall, the wall would cave in" (Nehemiah 4:3).

No matter what, there are going to be those forces who will seek to tear down, root up, and destroy God's kingdom (the Church). They are going to do whatever it takes to make sure that the Church falters in its mission (see Ephesians 6:12).

But Nehemiah shows us that when these enemy and defiant forces prey on us, that is the time to pray for them. Nehemiah prays in 4:4, "Hear us, O God, for we are despised." And this only reinforces what our forefathers used to say, "If I hold my peace and let the Lord fight my battle, victory shall be mine."

But not only did they face opposition from the outside, there were those on the inside who sought to spread discouragement among the people. As if the enemy from the outside was not enough to deal with, there is in every crowd faithless individuals on the inside of the camp who have no vision and seek to hinder the program by sowing seeds of discord, discouragement, and despair among the people. In short, they walk by sight and not by faith.

Yet, in spite of opposition from the outside and mutiny from the inside, the record declares that the walls were built in fifty-two days. Why? Because the people had a mind to work and Nehemiah had a strong determination that no matter what gets in the way, these walls were going to be rebuilt. I reiterate that Nehemiah was "too legit to quit."

A parallel exists between the days of Nehemiah and the times in which we live. For if we look closely at our world and the plight of our communities, we will discover that the walls are down, the gates are burned with fire, and the people are distressed and discouraged. When you see

- Adults acting like children and children acting like adults,
- The rich getting richer and the poor getting poorer,
- More black males in prison than in school,
- Abortion is the substitution for adoption,
- Patriotism takes precedence over racism,
- Television has taken the place of the family altar,
- The bar stool has taken the place of Bible study,
- Psychic advisors take the place of a prayerful attitude,
- 'Boyz' in the hood can't read, write, nor talk straight.

The walls are down, the gates are destroyed by fire, and the people are distressed and discouraged.

And I stopped by on my way to heaven to let you know that it's time for a rebuilding project. The walls of our community need to be rebuilt.

- The walls of renewal, reclamation, and reconciliation need to be rebuilt.
- The walls of family and moral values need to be rebuilt.
- The walls of love and justice need to be rebuilt.
- The walls of family and secret devotion need to be rebuilt.
- The walls of self-love and self-worth need to be rebuilt.
- The walls of Christian unity and brotherly love need to be rebuilt.

And the call is for us to stay on the wall until the job is done. Yes, there will be opposition, discouragements, distractions, those who will seek to delay and destroy our work (see John 16:33).

Yet, it is imperative that we stay on the wall. Don't give up, don't give in, don't throw in the towel for we are doing a great work that we cannot come down. We are "too legit to quit."

As I looked at Nehemiah's response, I needed to understand what would cause him to respond in this fashion. I needed to understand what would cause Nehemiah to leave the comfort of the palace, to leave financial security to return to a broken down city to rebuild its walls. In a day when missionaries are going AWOL from the mission station. In a day when the modem day prophet:

- is easily persuaded,
- is standing on shaky ground,
- priorities are questionable,
- has become a prophet for profit,
- when the agenda and vision of the modem-day prophet has been altered by economic expediency, political intimidation, and popular acclaim,

I needed to know what it was that caused Nehemiah to say, "I'm doing a great work so that I cannot come down."

I thought about this thing and I wondered if it was nostalgia. I wondered if it was a love for the return of the good old days? Was it a desire for the way things used to be that drove Nehemiah to return home?

I wondered if it was a desire for historical recognition. I wondered if it was a desire to leave his mark in the Jerusalem hall of fame. I wondered if he wanted to leave his name in the historical chronicles for years to come. But, no, it went far beyond that.

I thought about this thing and I discovered that there were three forces that motivated him and ought to motivate us.

A. A divine calling

And this calling is seen in two aspects. First, there is the calling to salvation. We have been called out of darkness into God's marvelous light. This is the concept behind the church. The word that is used for *church* in the Bible is the Greek word *ekklesia*, which means *to be called out from*. In other words, we have been called out from the world into a life of salvation in Jesus Christ. In other words, we are legit because of who we are in Christ Jesus. Who are we? We are the:

- saved, redeemed, sanctified, forgiven,
- twice born, children of the king,
- light of the world, salt of the earth,
- chosen generation, royal priesthood, peculiar people.

We are the ones whom God has picked up out of the muck and mire of sin and put us on a street called straight. We are a changed people, not on the outside, but changed on the inside. We are changed because we know that Christ in one's life does make a difference. And because He has come into our lives, we have a changed perspective. The things I used to do, I don't do anymore. The things I used to say, I don't say anymore. The places I used to go, I don't go anymore because Christ in one's life does make a difference. God has called us to a life of salvation.

Not only is there a calling to salvation, but there is also a calling to a life of service. God not only calls us to be saved, but He saves us that we might serve.

ILLUSTRATION: The calling of Isaiah and his answer.

APPLICATION: This is the kind of servant God wants. One who is willing to surrender his or her life totally to the Lord. One who is willing to say, "For God I'll live and for God I'll die." One who is willing to say, "Lord, I'm available to You."

I think I need to remind you that God is not looking for half-hearted servants. He wants our all. For Jesus said, "No man having put his hand to the plow and looking back is fit for the kingdom of God." I don't know about you, but if the Lord wants somebody, here am I, send me. We are legit because we have a divine calling.

B. A divine commission

Our commission is spelled out for us plainly in the Great Commission in Matthew 28:19-20. Now there are some of us who have a tendency of putting this Commission on an elite group of people, those whom, we feel, are trained to do this thing called "evangelism."

But the Scripture says, "Go ye . . ." This means that everyone that is twice born and blood washed has been given the responsibility to spread the message of the gospel into all the world. We are commissioned to go out into the highways and the hedges and compel me and women, boys and girls to come. You see, the lost have not moved, they are not going to move, and they are not going to come to us. We must go to them. We must go where they are and, in the words of Ezekiel 3:15, we must sit where they sit. We cannot be satisfied going to heaven without taking someone with us.

We need to tell our husband/wife/kids/niece/nephew/friend/enemy/coworker/employer/ that there is a God in heaven. He is alive and well and He offers salvation to all who would come to Him.

We need not be timid, for God is able to give us holy boldness through His spirit. We need not be fearful, for God has not given us the spirit of fear. We need not be worried about what to say for we have a relevant message to give to a dying world. We must tell them:

- There is a balm in Gilead to heal the sin-sick soul,
- God so loved the world . . .
- The wages of sin is death . . .
- God is still on the throne . . .
- There is a man from Galilee . . .

But don't just leave it at that, tell them your story. All of us have a story to tell, for God has brought us from somewhere. You can tell what He has done for you. If He's been your:

- Savior, Heart-fixer,
- Deliverer, Mind-regulator,
- Waymaker, Habit-breaker,

you ought to tell it. Let the redeemed of the Lord say so. I don't know about you, but I made it up in my mind that I'm going to tell it everywhere He blesses me to go!

C. A divine compulsion

There is an inner urging that motivates us. There is a greater power that moves us so that we march to the beat of a different drummer. History reveals to us those who were moved by a divine compulsion.

When religion was designed to keep us in the balcony and separated from others with no freedom of expression, there was a Richard Allen and an Absalom Jones who were moved by an inner urging to launch out into the deep and develop a movement relevant to the black experience.

When slavery kept our foreparents in chains physically, as well as psychologically, there was a Harriet Tubman who raised up and said, "Before I'd be a slave, I'll be buried in my grave; and go home to my Lord and be free."

When segregation kept us from the equalities that rightfully belonged to us, it was a Rosa Parks whose tired feet brought about a revolution for equality.

And we, like those before us, march to the beat of a different drummer. There is something on the inside that won't let me hold my peace.

- Jeremiah said it was like fire shut up in his bones,
- Ezekiel described it as a wheel in the middle of a wheel,
- Moses saw it as a burning bush that was not consumed,
- Luke detailed it as a mighty rushing wind,
- Somebody said, "Something got a hold of me . . ."
- Somebody said, "There is something within me I can't explain."

Zechariah said, ". . . not by power, nor by might, but by my Spirit, saith the Lord" (Zechariah 4:6). He makes you:

- cry when you ought to be smiling,
- laugh when the world is going to pieces,
- run when no one is chasing you,
- He gives you joy, unspeakable joy.

I act the way that I do because I can't help myself. God's Spirit is operating in me, with me, and through me. His anointing is upon me and is at work in my life. You can't help but move in power when the anointing is upon you. When the anointing is upon you:

- go where He wants you to go,
- do what He wants you to do,
- say what He wants you to say.

The anointing does make a difference!

CONCLUSION

You may be facing difficult times in your life. You may be at the point where you are wondering, "Is it worth it?" You may be at the end of your rope and feel like calling it quits. But I want to encourage you to stay on the wall.

- Folk may talk about you,
- Folk may ridicule you,
- Folk may use and misuse you,

- Folk may call you everything but a child of God, but stay on the wall.

For the Scripture says:

- Galatians 6:9: "Let us not be weary in well doing, for in due season you shall reap if you faint not."
- James 1:12: "Blessed is the man that endures temptation; for when he is tried, he shall receive the crown of life."
- Revelation 2:10: "Be thou faithful unto death, and I will give you a crown of life."
- 1 Corinthians 15:58: ". . . be steadfast, unmovable, always abounding in the work of the Lord; forasmuch as ye know that your labor is not in vain in the Lord."

I've made it up in my mind that I'm going to stay on the wall. I'm going to work until my day is done. I'm going to hold on to God's unchanging hand. For:

> If when you give the best of your service,
> Telling the world that the Savior has come;
> Be not dismayed when men don't believe you,
> He understands; He'll say, "Well done."
> Oh, when I come to the end of my journey,
> Weary of life and the battle is won;
> Carrying the staff and the cross of redemption,
> He'll understand, and say, "Well done."

FROM A MESS TO A MESSAGE

And they arrived at the country of the Gadarenes, which is over against Galilee. And when he went forth to land, there met him out of the city a certain man, which had devils long time, and ware no clothes, neither abode in any house, but in the tombs. When he saw Jesus, he cried out, and fell down before him, and with a loud voice said, "What have I to do with thee, Jesus, thou Son of God most high? I beseech thee, torment me not." (For he had commanded the unclean spirit to come out of the man. For oftentimes it had caught him: and he was kept bound with chains and in fetters; and he brake the bands, and was driven of the devil into the wilderness.)

And Jesus asked him, saying, "What is thy name?" And he said, "Legion," because many devils were entered into him. And they besought him that he would not command them to go out into the deep. And there was there an herd of many swine feeding on the mountain: and they besought him that he would suffer them to enter into them. And he suffered them. Then went the devils out of the man, and entered into the swine: and the herd ran violently down a steep place into the lake, and were choked.

When they that fed them saw what was done, they fled, and went and told it in the city and in the country. Then they went out to see what was done; and came to Jesus, and found the man, out of whom the devils were departed, sitting at the feet of Jesus, clothed, and in his right mind: and they were afraid. They also which saw it told them by what means he that was possessed of the devils was healed. Then the whole multitude of the country of the Gadarenes round about besought him to depart from them; for they were taken with great fear: and he went up into the ship, and returned back again.

Now the man out of whom the devils were departed besought him that he might be with him: but Jesus sent him away, saying, "Return to thine own house, and shew how great things God hath done unto thee." And he went his way, and published throughout the whole city how great things Jesus had done unto him (Luke 8:26-39).

One of the readings that have profoundly influenced my thinking is a book written by Jonathan Kozel entitled *Amazing Grace*. In this book, this Jewish writer raises the issue of the value of life by looking at life in the inner city, in particular, in the South Bronx section of New York. In relating his experiences of interviewing those who ministered as well as those who were ministered to, the book raises the question that must be considered for all intents and purposes. Is the world that we live in only for the privileged or is all life valuable? To put it another way, are the have-nots of society expendable or does the salvation of one person really make a difference?

If this question were posed to Jesus, He would tell us that all life is precious. One of the more unique aspects of the ministry of Jesus was the inclusiveness of His ministry. His ministry moved across the traditional boundaries in order to reach people. He reached people wherever they were in order to move them where they needed to be.

- He ministered to Nicodemus, a Pharisee; yet, He also broke with the tradition of the day and spoke with the woman at Jacob's well.
- He healed the daughter of Jairus, a ruler of the synagogue; yet, He also healed the woman who had the issue of blood for twelve long years.
- He dined at the house of Simon the Pharisee; yet, He also dined at the house of Simon the leper.

Jesus was equal opportunity in His ministry. He sought to be the all-inclusive Savior in order to move a person from where they were to where they needed to be.

Despite the fact that He ministered equally to all, biblical evidence suggests that Jesus had an affinity for those who lived on the margins of life—those of whom the late African American theologian, Howard Thurman, referred to as the disinherited—those whose backs are against the wall. Jesus had a habit of ministering to those who were the marginalized of society.

What does it mean to live on the margins? To live on the margins means that:

- you are tagged or labeled as a minority.
- you are excluded from the mainstream of society.
- you are disenfranchised, not afforded the opportunities that the privileged are exposed to.
- you are branded as a misfit and treated as an outcast.
- you are treated as a menace to society.
- you are a statistic to the mainstream of society.
- you are victimized by racism, classism, and sexism.
- you are subject to racial profiling,
- you are in a situation, not of your own accord, but because society has placed you there.
- you are living but no one cares whether or not you are alive.

Now there are those who adhere to the bootstrap theory. I hear what you are saying, "I pulled myself up by my own bootstraps. After all, God helps those who help themselves." However, the last time I checked my Bible, and I checked it this morning, I'm told that God helps those who cannot help themselves.

That's why Jesus came. His mission, His concern, and His passion were for the weak and the suffering. He was concerned for those who were disenfranchised—who were deprived of the privileges of life. He had compassion for those whose lives were a mess. He had compassion on those who could not help themselves. He openly said:

- that those who are well do not need a physician, only those who are sick.
- that He came to seek and to save that which was lost.
- that He came to those who were the least of these.
- that He came to minister to those whose lived life on the margins.

His personal mission statement verified that His ministry reached beyond the realm of the privileged to the underprivileged (see Luke 4:18-19). Christ came to reach those who lived on the margins whose lives were in a mess, to give them peace, purpose, and a passion.

Such is the case as is revealed in this scenario of the life of Jesus. One of the more famous missions of Jesus was to reach a single, solitary man. Jesus spent only a few hours in this region yet, when He left, He made an indelible impression on a young man's life. Why? Because God is no respecter of persons. All are precious in the sight of the Savior.

This scenario takes place in the Decapolis, a predominately Gentile region of ten cities. It is interesting to note that this is the first time during His ministry that Jesus has crossed over the Sea of Galilee into this region known as Gadara. Jesus had already told His disciples to cross over to the other side, but there was more to this than what meets the eye. This was a geographical crossing, yes, but it was more than geographical. When Jesus crosses the Sea of Galilee to the region of the Gadarenes:

- He crosses over to those who are not of the covenant.
- He crosses over to those who are not Jewish by descent.
- He crosses the cultural and religious boundaries, to share time and space with those who, according to Jewish standards, were impure and unclean.
- He crosses the boundaries to reach those who needed the salvific, liberating message of the kingdom of God.

As soon as Jesus crosses the sea, He encounters one who is living on the margins—who is in a messed up condition. Look at who this young man was. Psychiatrists and psychologists would have us believe that this man was mentally challenged or emotionally unstable. However, Luke, in giving us the resume of this man, informs us that he was demon possessed. This was not your average possession case. No! This demon had this young man so messed up that he didn't know who he was. When asked what his name was, this young man did not speak. No! The demon spoke through him, "My name is Legion for we are many."

A legion was a Roman regiment of about 6,000 men. Here is this man in a messed up situation with 6,000 demons living in him.

There are three things that are noted concerning this no-named individual. This man was a terror to the community. To some, he was considered a menace to society. The authorities tried to keep him tied up. They tried to keep him incarcerated but he could not be contained, but with the strength that only insane people possess, he would break the chains and go streaking through the night.

- Streaking through the neighborhoods,
- Streaking through the parks,
- Streaking around the corners terrorizing the community.

He was also a terror to himself—he endured untold misery, which sought relief in screams and self-inflicted torture. Nobody knew the inner hell that this man was experiencing. Nobody knew what this man was going through. He would go off for days; no one would know where he was. With fierce cries that made the rocks and mountains ring with the expression of his agony, the Bible says that he would cut himself with stones. He would victimize himself with self-inflicted wounds. He would mutilate himself. He had no hope, no peace, no joy, no purpose, so he would try to kill himself.

Furthermore, he had an unusual place of residence. This individual was living among the tombs. The tombs were isolated burial grounds that were cut out of the cliffs and were avoided by many people The tombs were caves that afforded refuge for despots and those who were the outcasts of society. The tombs were places of hopelessness.

Why was this man living in the tombs? I looked at this and I discovered that he made his residence in the tombs because the people had given up on him. He wasn't worth the time and effort to move him to responsible living. So, we'll place him out there in the tombs. And as long as he is out there, we know we've got it under control.

Imagine the disgrace of the family. Imagine the frustration of his friends who could do nothing with him. And there he is on the margins of life with no one to care and nowhere to go, unable to be controlled, living among the destitute and the outcasts of society. This no-name individual was in a mess and spent his life in a hopeless, helpless, hapless, hideous, messed up condition.

But early one morning, he meets a man who had just got off of a boat from a midnight journey across the sea. This man was named Jesus. When Jesus gets off the boat, this man sees Him from a distance. He pauses, gazes, and approaches Jesus. Upon recognizing who He is, he falls down at His feet and the demons in this man cry out with a loud voice, "What have you to do with me, Jesus of Nazareth, Son of the Most High God? Have you come to torment us?"

Even demons worship and tremble at the name of Jesus. If they tremble at His name, what do they do in His presence? The demons fall before Jesus as a sign of reverence and submission. That's a defensive posture—because they know they are in the presence of One who is more powerful than they. They know their time is limited. They know their ultimate fate. They know that the abyss, their place of confinement, was prepared for them. But they were not ready for this. So what did they do? They began to bargain with Jesus.

"Come here, Jesus. I don't know why you are messing with us now. You're messing with our game plan. So let's make a deal."

On the mountainside, not very far away, there was a herd of swine, about 2,000 of them, feeding. These demons requested permission to enter these swine.

Jesus didn't command it, He permitted it. He granted them permission. Immediately, they left the man and entered the swine. These swine ran frantically down the hillside into the sea and were drowned.

The demons thought they had Jesus licked. They were looking for a way to destroy His testimony in the city. They thought themselves to be victorious. But Jesus,

- being the God-human,
- being the omniscient One,
- being the all-knowing One,

knew what they were trying to do. Demons cannot mess with the Master of all.

This news spread like wildfire. The gossip line was on fire. The Negro-net was flowing. Everybody heard what had happened. The people of the community came to see what was going on, but when they arrived, they saw this man,

- who lived on the margins of life,
- who was cutting himself with stones,
- who would scream out in agony day in and day out,

sitting at the feet of Jesus, clothed and in his right mind. And Luke declares that the people were afraid. I couldn't help but wonder why the people were afraid.

- When he was ranting and raving they were not afraid, but now that he is sitting, they are afraid.

- When he was naked they were not afraid, but now he is fully dressed and they are afraid.
- When he was crazy they were not afraid, but now that he is in his right mind, they are afraid.

But now, they are afraid. What were they afraid of? I don't know.

A. Maybe they were afraid of further economic loss to themselves. Maybe they were afraid because of the economic disaster that this caused. For there are always people who are more concerned about money that they are about souls for the kingdom.

B. Maybe they were afraid of the change. They were comfortable with the man out there in the tombs. As long as they had him in the tombs, they could deal with him. But people have a hard time dealing with change. This man had been arrested by the power of God and moved to responsible living.

C. Maybe they were afraid of the power of God at work in their midst. Maybe they were afraid of the supernatural. For this story is a paradigm of what happens when Christ comes into a life. He is able to change your attitude. He is able to change your address from:

- Dead Alley to Dignity Street.
- Shameful Road to Self-esteem Drive.
- Disgrace Lane to Self-respect Blvd.

"What a wonderful change in my life has been wrought since Jesus came into my heart!" There were two requests—when you read this passage you will find two requests.

1. There was the request made by the townspeople. They requested that Jesus would leave their community. What a sad scenario:

- Instead of rejoicing over this transformation that had taken place in the life of this man, they were more concerned about the economics.
- Instead of being concerned over the change that has taken place in a man's life, they were more concerned about dealing with the changes they had to make.

Can you imagine anybody asking Jesus to leave their community?

2. There was the request of the young man. He begs Jesus to allow him to go with Him. "Jesus, I want to go with you. Jesus, I want to go where you are going." But Jesus tells him to go home and tell the people what great things God has done for you. Why? Because it was God, who took this man's mess and gave him a message. And Jesus will not be left without a witness.

CONCLUSION

Is there anybody here who has been in a mess? Is there anybody here who has been in hopeless situations?

- Your household was in a mess,

- Your health was in a mess,
- Your marriage was in a mess,
- Your finances were in a mess,
- Your life was in a mess.

But God took your mess and turned it into a message! He gave you a testimony! What is that message? It's a message of:

- salvation/deliverance/liberation,
- hope in the midst of hopelessness,
- sight in the midst of blindness,
- holiness in the midst of hellishness,
- faith in the midst of frustration.

What is that message? "Can't nobody do me like Jesus." Can't nobody do you like Jesus? "I'm so glad Jesus lifted me."

GET OUT OF THE WINDOW

"Seated in a window was a young man named Eutychus, who was sinking into a deep sleep as Paul talked on and on. When he was sound asleep, he fell to the ground from the third story and was picked up dead" (Acts 20:7-12).

It's amazing how God speaks to us through the various situations we experience in life. It's amazing how the Spirit of God uses life experiences to teach us timeless principles through the word of God.

The topic under consideration was born out of one of those life experiences. It was a warm, summer day a few years ago. We were spending time with some family out of town. As the day was drawing to a close, we were standing outside, saying our final good-byes before returning home. In the midst of our conversation, there was a young girl around five years of age who lived next door. She had opened the window and was sitting on the ledge of this upstairs window. There was no screen in the window and there was no parental guidance in the room. Instinctively, someone who knew the girl warned her to get out of the window before she fell out and hurt herself. After a few tense moments, this child backed away from the window and returned to her normal routine of playing.

If this child had not been warned to get out of the window, she would have continued to flirt with danger and could have been fatally injured.

This incident from our personal chronicles brought to light this historical narrative from the book of Acts. Paul was on his third missionary journey. It was the first day of the week. The disciples were gathered together, as was their custom, for the breaking of bread; i.e. observing the Lord's Supper. He was in Troas and was intending to leave on the following day for the next city.

During this time of worship, Paul preached, and he preached, and he preached. In fact, he preached until midnight. The room where they were gathered was crowded and there were many lights in the room.

As Paul continued to preach, a young lad by the name of Eutychus, who was somewhere between the ages of 8 and 14, was tired and fell asleep. What is so significant is not that Eutychus fell asleep, but where he fell asleep. Eutychus fell asleep in a window that was located in the third loft of the house. This window was a lattice opening for the sake of air in a crowded room. As he sat in a deep sleep in this window in the third loft of this house, the Bible declares that he fell out of the window and was taken up dead. Imagine the rising sobs and the wailings of people around him. Imagine the shock of parents, family, and friends as they stood around in disbelief over this tragedy. Imagine the agony within the hearts of the parents who loved him so dearly. This was a tragedy that no one could not be affected by.

But Paul immediately went to the young lad, fell on him and embraced him. Then he reassured everyone present not to worry, for life was still in him.

They continued in the breaking of bread and Paul continued preaching even until the morning. When he completed his discourse, he left for the next city. But, the miracle of this scenario is seen in the life of Eutychus. This young lad

- who became tired in the church service,
- who had fallen asleep in the window in the third loft,
- who has also fallen out of this window from the third loft,

was taken home alive. And the Bible declares that there was great joy and comfort.

An incident such as this is all too familiar to us. How many times have we heard the news of children falling out of windows? How many times have we witnessed the agony and distress of parents and family, as well as, the disbelief and concern of a community over a child who played too close to the ledge of the window or balcony? This is a tragic scenario in our society.

But, if you will, allow me to suggest that the tragedy of this reality cannot be looked at just in a literal sense. For figuratively, there are many children and youth and young adults who are sitting on the ledge of the windows in the church. They are in the church physically, but mentally and emotionally, they are outside of the church. They are in the church, they know what is going on in the church, yet they are disinterested, dissatisfied, and disgruntled, simply because the church has not provided a relevant ministry to address the realities they are experiencing. And unlike the personal experience I just shared with you, it seems as if no one takes any real concern or interest in them until after they have fallen out of the window.

It is no secret that we are losing our youth at a rapid rate. Every day we hear of the tragic situations that many of our youth find themselves in. According to the Children's Defense Fund in Washington, D.C., every day in the United States

- 2,781 teenage girls get pregnant,
- 1,115 teenage girls have abortions,
- 1,295 teenage girls give birth,
- 2,556 children are born out of wedlock,
- 4,219 teenagers contract sexually-transmitted diseases,
- 5,314 teenagers are arrested,
- 135,000 children bring a gun to school.

I am convinced that now, more than ever, the church can ill-afford to do business as usual. This passage in Acts suggests that we can become so involved in having church that we forget to be the church. There is more to church than having church. We must be involved in the building of the lives of men, women, boys, and girls so that we can change a generation.

I looked at this passage and there were some things that troubled me. Every now and then we need to raise questions of the text so that we can develop a clear understanding of the text.

One of the questions that I raised of this narrative by Luke is: Why was Eutychus, this boy somewhere between the ages of 8 and 14, in the window in the first place? It just seems to me that if you have a child that age, you would not want him sitting in anyone's window.

This suggests that we can ill-afford to be out of touch with the needs of our youth. Robert Murray of Norfolk, VA, stated that "the church has, in some cases, abandoned our children and has failed to minister to them. We have excluded them from our ministries."

When we neglect the youth as well as the young adults, they can fall out of the window of the church house and

- fall into the window of the crack house,

- fall into the window of the jail house,
- fall into the window of illicit relationships,
- fall into the window of other forms of religious expression.

God did not make our children to be crack addicts and alcoholics, gangsters and gang-bangers, murderers and thugs, pimps and prostitutes. God made our children to be liberators of a generation. As the Word Incarnate becomes alive in them, they can become instruments in the hands of God to bring a message of liberation to those who are in bondage.

The other question that perplexed me was: What caused Eutychus to fall asleep? You can't put the blame of Eutychus for falling asleep. The Scripture tells us of three things that caused him to fall asleep in the window:

1) Luke is sure to let us know that there were many lights in this upper room. These lights were oil lamps. Anyone familiar with oil lamps know that when these lamps are burning, they let out fumes, which, if you are not careful, can cause drowsiness to come upon you.

2) The crowded conditions in the house caused this room to be quite warm and un-comfortable. This upper room was crowded to hear this persecutor turned preacher. Since we know that heat rises and that we draw heat, the room was apparently quite uncomfortable.

3) The lateness of the hour. It was midnight and Paul was still preaching strong. And at midnight with the high heat and high fumes, Eutychus fell asleep.

This suggests to us that we can become so involved in having church that we neglect the ministry to the children. I don't mean any harm but I am of the persuasion that the church must forgo the mentality that the youth are the church of tomorrow. They are the church of today. How can we say that our children are the church of tomorrow when tomorrow is not promised to us? How can we say that they are the church of tomorrow when they are present here and now?

In examining this passage, I found that it gives some timeless principles as we seek to minister to the youth of our church and our community.

A. We must take an active interest in the lives of our children.

Eutychus is sitting in the window, asleep in the window and, subsequently, falls out of the window. What is it that causes the Eutychuses of this age to fall asleep and fall out of the window of the church?

For one thing, what was going on really doesn't interest them. The church does seem to be addressing the issues that need to be addressed in their lives. They feel the church is irrelevant and out of touch. Thus, the church is boring and uninteresting to them, thus of no intrinsic value to them.

Second, they are tired of the hypocrisy in some adults. When they look at some of the saints, they see a contradiction between what is said in the church and what is done in the community. The very things that many of us severely condemn are the things we are actually doing ourselves.

Eutychus should have never been in the window in the first place. He would not have been there if someone had just recognized what was going on.

The church must recognize where they are and do something about it. We must move them out of the window. We must move them from the place of danger to the place where they also can receive a blessing. They need to know that we care, in spite of the upheaval that takes place in many of their lives. They need to see from the church that we genuinely love them and are concerned about them. If they don't hear it from us, they will hear it from someone else.

B. We must seek to catch them before they fall. We cannot wait until they have fallen to show concern.

When Eutychus fell out of the window, everyone left their position to huddle around him. Listen to the concerns of the people. "Is he dead? What happened? How could this happen to him?" They were so concerned with being in church that they neglected Eutychus in the window.

Too often, no one pays any attention to the Eutychuses of today until they have fallen out of the window. Once they have fallen, people feel powerless to save them.

Once our children have fallen, some become judge and jury and begin the condemnation process. "They shouldn't have been in the window in the first place. They knew the dangers. They knew better." Rather than:

- constructing, they are criticizing,
- delivering, they are destroying,
- building up, they are tearing down.

Too often the church is guilty of reacting to what has happened rather than being proactive and seeking a preventive cure. The church must be willing to deal with these issues that are confronting our youth before they really begin to deal with them. The church must be proactive in its ministry.

C. If they do fall, we must seek to revive and restore them to wholesome, productive living.

It's one thing to fall down, but it's another to stay down. When Eutychus fell and they saw he was dead, Paul took an immediate concern for his life. He felt and knew in his spirit that it wasn't too late. Even though the situation looked bleak and hopeless, all was not lost. Luke shows three things that Paul did.

1) Paul went down to him,
2) Paul fell on him,
3) Paul embraced him.

Our children can be saved. There is hope for them to be saved, revived, and restored. We must let them know that God cares through us. We should never give up on them. Why? Because there were some folk who were ready to give up on you. They said you were nothing and would never amount to anything. But somebody prayed for you. Some sainted mother, some godly father, some redeemed grandmother prayed for you. They invested time in you and look where you are today. You're still holding on to God's unchanging hand.

Paul went to where Eutychus was. He wasn't afraid to get to where he was for he recognized that this soul was more important than his personal protection. Paul fell on him and embraced him. It was the embrace of Paul that changed the course of Eutychus' life forever. Paul understood the pressures, the challenges, and the pain. Paul took the time to embrace, to influence his life, and through an embrace, Paul took a seemingly hopeless life and restored it to productive life. Here, the miracle was performed.

When a life is restored, that's a miracle. When a life is saved from destruction, that's a miracle. God is still in the miracle-working business!

If we are to win the souls of young people to Christ, we must be willing to invest some serious time into their lives. We must be transparent. We must be willing to give our testimony and be open with them. We must be willing to admit our faults of the past and show them that through God's grace, God took our stumbling blocks and turned them into stepping stones.

We must do this because the same thing that Paul did for Eutychus, that's what God, in Christ, did for us.

- He left the heights of glory to walk upon the earth,
- He descended from Godhood to dwell in manhood,
- He descended from exaltation to dwell in humiliation.

That's the message of the cross!

LESSONS FROM THE TOWEL [10]

"So he got up from the meal, took off his outer clothing, and wrapped a towel around his waist. After that, he poured water into a basin and began to wash his disciples' feet, drying them with the towel that was wrapped around him"
(John 13:1-17 NIV).

Great lessons come from the most unlikely sources. Life is so designed that the simple tasks in one's life can birth some of the greatest truths. Many of us will attest to the fact that it doesn't take God much to accomplish His purposes. God can use the little insignificant things of life to teach us great and valuable lessons.

Such is the case from John's account of the life of Jesus. In this historical narrative, we see a visible parable of Kingdom expectations. Jesus is teaching a master principle of ministry and of church leadership, which all of us must equally face. The principle to be learned is that true greatness is not found in coaxing or inducing others to serve you, but giving yourself in service to others. This is what is known as servant leadership. Those who are nearest and dearest to the heart of Christ imitate His habits, especially in the area of practical servanthood.

It is important to remember that servant leadership is always redemptive. That is, it is never without cost, but involves voluntarily taking up the cross (see Luke 9:23). It requires that you and I become inconvenienced for the sake of someone else. If what I am doing, in the name of the cross, is not healing someone or making life better for someone else, then it does not qualify as servant leadership.

Jesus focuses on this issue because, like so many other things, Jesus had spent three and a half years teaching His disciples specific concepts regarding the Kingdom. And, even though Jesus had poured His whole life into them, these Kingdom principles still had not worked their way into their lives, especially when it related to the issue of servanthood. He had told them time and time again the importance of being a servant in the Father's eyes. He said,

- "Whoever would be great among you shall be your minister"(Matthew 20:26);
- "Whoever of you will be chief, shall be servant of all" (Mark 10:44);
- "He who finds his life shall lose it, and he who loses his life shall find it" (Matthew 10:39);
- "The first shall be last and the last shall be first" (Matthew 20:16);
- "He did not come to be served, but to serve and give his life as a ransom for many" (Matthew 20:28).

And after all of this teaching about a servant, they still didn't get it. They were flunking Servanthood 101. How do we know that? We know this because several times Jesus had to dispel their ideas regarding servanthood. Their idea of leadership was only driven by what they had witnessed

---

[10]This sermon was preached during Passion Week services.

among the Pharisees. The disciples were thinking about seats and Jesus was thinking about service. This idea was only compounded by what was presently taking place.

In order to understand this text, you must understand the customs of that day. Foot washing was a common custom of this time. The roads of Palestine were dirt roads and designer sandals were the footwear of the day. In dry weather, they were inches deep in dust. But, in wet weather, they walked in inches of mud. When one entered the house, they would remove their sandals and there were always great water pots provided at the door to wash one's feet. In the wealthier households, a servant was there with a pitcher and a towel to wash the soiled feet of the guests.

But not on this occasion. This was not a wealthy household. The custom was that the last one in the room was the designated foot-washer, the one who was to wash the feet of all who were present. And, after all the arguments and disputes among the disciples about who would be the greatest in the Kingdom, Jesus sensed the need to go one step further in his teaching. So, He moved from:

- didache to demonstration,
- from proclamation to practice,
- from instruction to illustration,
- from education to example.

Jesus decided to preach an illustrative sermon to His disciples. What did He do? The master became a slave. The highest took on the lowest estate. Come with me as we go into the upper room with Jesus. Look at what is happening. He gets up, disrobes himself, wraps himself in a towel, pours water in a basin, and begins to wash the feet of His disciples and dry their feet with the towel He is wrapped in.

Imagine the shock and disbelief in the minds of the disciples. Imagine the stunned look and the humiliation they felt as He went from one to another. Imagine the silence as He goes around the room. Not a word from anyone. The only sound you hear is the splashing of water as He washed their feet.

- From Andrew to James and John.
- From Bartholemew to Matthew and Thomas.
- From Judas and Thaddeus to Philip, James, the son of Alphaeus and Simon the Zealot.
- Yes, even to Peter.

Perhaps, in the name of the group, Simon Peter registered his verbal protest of the matter: "No, Master, I can't let you wash my feet. Remember, I'm the one who came walking to you on the water. I'm the one who let down his net at your word and caught a great catch of fish. I'm the one who said you were the Christ, the Son of the living God. You're my revered leader and I cannot let you wash my feet."

Jesus said to him in a soft, concerned tone, "If you fail to submit to this act of humility, you will miss the whole concept of the Kingdom's operation. You will be excluded from the unfolding plan of divine revelation. If you do not let me wash your feet, you will have no part with me."

And Peter, just like so many of us, jumps from one extreme to another. "Lord, not just my feet, but wash my head, wash my whole body." Jesus said, "If you have been washed one time, you do not need to be washed again, except to wash your feet." After completing this task, He rises, puts his clothes on, sits down. Then He speaks to them.

> "Do you understand what I have done for you? You call me teacher and Lord,
> and you are right in doing so for that's what I am. If, then, your Lord and
> teacher, has washed your feet, you ought to wash one another's feet. For I
> have set you an example that you should do as I have done for you."

Jesus, washing the feet of His disciples, was a spiritual lesson using the medium of visual aid. What was Jesus trying to tell His disciples? What was Jesus really saying in demonstrating this sermon to us?

In preaching this illustrative sermon, He demonstrated the proper motive for service in the kingdom of God. What is the proper motive? It is love. The Bible declares that He loved His disciples very dearly. In fact, it says that He was preparing to show them the full extent of His love.

You cannot truly serve anyone unless you have a genuine love for God's people. Paul said, "Though I speak with the tongues of men and of angels and do not have love, I am as sounding brass or a tinkling cymbal" (1 Corinthians 13:1). Regardless of who they are and where they have come from, service in the kingdom of God means loving your neighbor.

- They may not look like you do,
- They may not act like you do,
- They may not think like you do,
- They may have some faults about them,

but we learn to love them. We may not love their ways, but we love them. We love them because we love Him, and we love Him because He first loved us.

One thing that has been lost within the historic church is the genuine care that we once had for all people. There was a time when there was somebody who lived in the community of faith would rally around and see to it that the need was met. Do we not need to recapture this demonstrative love within the faith community? Do we not need to recapture that love that runs from heart to heart and from breast to breast?

Paul in Colossians calls love the bond of perfectness. Love is the superglue that holds all things together. In fact, James says that love covers a multitude of sins. And true service, true leadership must operate in the realm of love. A love that is not talked about, but a love that is demonstrated in our daily lives.

In this illustrative sermon that Jesus preached on that Thursday night, He was letting us know that as we serve, we will come in contact with various people to whom we are to minister.

You will notice that Jesus went to each of His disciples. He did not leave one out. He did not skip over Bartholomew to get to Peter or Thaddeus to get to John. He washed the feet of each one of His disciples. In doing this, He is letting us know that they represent the very ones we are called upon to minister to.

One of the concepts that ministry teaches us is that you cannot be selective in whom you serve. One of the tragedies of the modem Christian experience is that we are guilty of ministry segregation. We want to minister to those who will not take us out of our comfort zones. In other words, we want the crown, but not the cross.

But, the reality of the matter is, we are called upon to minister to those who don't have it all together. You are going to be called upon to minister to those

- Peters who always put their foot in their big mouths, who will claim loyalty to you but will eventually deny you.
- James and Johns whose main focus is jockeying for position and power.
- Nathaneals who have hidden prejudices in their lives and won't say anything until they are confronted.
- Thomases who will question everything you do and will doubt your genuineness until they can see it for themselves.
- Matthews who have stolen from you and cheated you.
- Bartholomews who have power but don't know what to do with it.
- Judases who will smile in your face one minute and turn around and betray you the next minute.

You will be called upon to minister to folk who may not like you just because you are who you are.

But Jesus washed their feet. And, as He washed their feet, He came in contact with all the stuff they came in contact with as they walked along the dusty roads and through the fields. This shows us that servants cannot be afraid to get their hands dirty.

I cannot help but wonder: If the towel could talk, what would it say? I hear the towel saying, "I know you. I know who you are. I know where you have been. I've seen where your feet have been. You've been places you should not have gone. You've dealt with faces you shouldn't have dealt with. You've had to run from some situations you shouldn't have been in the first place." The towel says, "I know you."

But, who's holding the towel?

The last thing that Jesus said is that true greatness in the minds of the disciples differed sharply from what was in the mind and heart of Jesus. He knew that He was a king and did not need external pomp and splendor to demonstrate it. While the disciples were jockeying for the best seat in the house, Jesus was the only one to take up the towel. This was His way of saying that true greatness does not lie in:

- social prestige,
- your social, economic, or political background,
- your pedigree or your degree.

True greatness lies in taking up the towel.

- It lies in service,
- it lies in giving,
- it lies in sharing,
- it lies in taking up the cross.

We see Jesus giving Himself for humanity, for He took up the towel for us, and said, "I did not come to be served, but to serve and to give my life as a ransom for many." He served us and gave His life so that you and I could have a right to the tree of life. He **died**:

- until death died,
- the moon dripped in blood,
- the sun refused to shine,
- the earth trembled.

He served us:

- by serving as our sinless substitute,
- by serving as our sacrificial Lamb,
- by becoming sin for us,
- by securing forgiveness for us,
- by taking our sins and giving us his righteousness,
- by securing our salvation!

I PUT IT ALL IN HIS HANDS[11]

"Father, into thy hands I commend my spirit" (Luke 23:46).

These words make up our Lord's final utterance from the cross of Calvary. For six long and dreadful hours, Jesus

- experienced the agony and the excruciating pain of a cruel Roman death penalty,
- made His soul an offering for sin and gave His life as a ransom for many,
- was suspended between heaven and hell, not by the nails in His hands, but by bands of love.

And now, the dreadful ordeal of the soul being over, He breathes His last utterance quoting David's words in Psalm 31, "Father into thy hands I commend my spirit."

This was our Lord's seventh utterance from the cross. The number seven in Scripture is significant, for it is the number of completeness or perfection. You will recall that in six days God created the world and all that was in it, and, on the seventh day, He rested. So Jesus, the work being given to him to reconcile the world back to God, completed His work. So the seventh utterance brings him to the place of rest in the Father's hands. Hence, He cries out with a loud voice a prayer that every Hebrew child was taught when their mothers tucked them in for the night, "Father, into thy hands I commend my spirit."

This word, this utterance, speaks of our Savior back in communion with the Father. Having taken upon himself the sin of the world, having become sin for us, God the Father withdrew Himself from God the Son as the sword of divine judgment fell upon Him. Having become our sin-bearer, paying redemption's price and experiencing separation from the Father, He is now back in communion with the Father and cries out, "Father, into thy hands I commend my spirit."

These words, according to one writer, were our Lord's entrance greeting into heaven. He had spent twelve hours in the hands of sinful men. Twelve hours of:

- revilement and ridicule,
- pain and parody,
- misrepresentation and mockery.

And, now, He commits, He dismisses His spirit into the hands of the Father by speaking His final conviction about life and its meaning, "Father, into thy hands I comment my spirit."

I want to suggest to you that He put it all in the Father's hands.

And what a lesson we need to learn today. We must learn to put everything into the hands of God. What am I talking about? I'm talking about putting our lives, burdens, problems, troubles, cares, difficulties, anxieties, frustrations, yesterdays, todays and tomorrows

in the Father's hands.

We spend all of our lives in someone else's hands.

---

[11]This sermon was prepared and preached for Good Friday services for the Women's Department of the Allegheny Union Baptist Association at the Monumental Baptist Church in Pittsburgh.

- From the doctor's hands, we go to the nurse's hands,
- From the nurse's hands, we go to our parent's hands,
- From our parent's hands, we go to the teacher's hands,
- From the teacher's hands, we go to the employer's hands,
- From the employer's hands, we go to our spouse's hands,
- From our spouse's hands, we go back to the doctor and the nurse's hands,
- From the doctor's and the nurse's hands, we go to the mortician's hands,
- From the mortician's hands, we go to the hands of Him who created all things!

How much more, then, should we place our lives in the Father's hands. For the Scripture says,

- "Casting your cares upon Him, for He cares for you" (1 Peter 5:7);
- "Cast thy burdens upon the Lord and he will sustain you, He will never suffer the righteous to be moved" (Psalm 55:22);
- "Be anxious for nothing, but in everything, by prayer and supplication, with thanksgiving, let your request be made known unto God" (Philippians 4:6).

We must learn to put it all in the Father's hands.

How much better off we would be if we would learn to put everything in His hands. How much trouble, how many heartaches and pains we would have saved ourselves if we would have placed things in His hands. How often have we tried to do our own thing? How often have we tried:

- to heal a heartache
- to bear a burden
- to alleviate anxiety in our own power.

I know what it's like. I know what it's like to have a molehill turn into a mountain because I had not put things in His hands. I know what it's like to have harmless situations turn into to shameful and painful embarrassments by not placing them in His hands. I know what it's like to see insignificant trials turn into sizable disappointments because I had not placed them in the Father's hands.

You know what I am talking about. You know what it was like when you thought you had all the answers to all the questions. You know what it was like when you thought you had the solution to the problem. You know what it was like when you thought you had the cure for the catastrophe, only to discover that you were trying to answer the wrong questions.

But, when you placed things in His hands, He demonstrated His power by bringing that thing to pass. When you placed it in His hands, He demonstrated His power by working things out for you. When you placed it in His hands, He made a way out of no way. When you placed it in His hands, you found Him to be:

- the Healer of your heartache,
- the Savior of your soul,
- the Source of your strength,
- the Liberator of your life,
- the Supplier of your every need, and,
- the Giver of every good and perfect gift.

And on the strength of God's goodness, your testimony echoes that of our Lord Jesus, "Father, into thy hands I commend my spirit." I put it all in His hands.

This seventh utterance from the cross, this prayer of Christ, suggests:

A. Relationship: "Father . . ."

This suggests to us that there is familiarity, friendship, and intimacy between Jesus and the Father. In other words, Jesus is placing His spirit in the hands of someone He knows. For between He and the Father was a long and cherished history. Jesus knew who He was dealing with for there was a close relationship between He and the Father. So close was this relationship that Jesus Himself testified, "I and the Father are one" (John 10:30).

It's dangerous placing your life in the hands of someone you do not know. It's dangerous placing your life in unfriendly and unfamiliar hands. History is replete with those whose lives have been destroyed or altered because of unfamiliar and unfriendly hands.

- Sisera ended up in the unfamiliar hands of Jael and lost the battle as well as his life,
- Samson ended up in the unfamiliar hands of Delilah and lost his strength,

It's dangerous trusting your life to someone you do not know. It was unfamiliar hands that:

- slapped and scorned Jesus,
- cursed and crucified Jesus,
- reviled and ridiculed Jesus.

It's dangerous placing your life in unfamiliar hands!

But, Jesus says, "Father . . .," for on the cross Jesus did not make a heavenly hypothesis, a cosmic conjecture, or an eternal supposition. He knew who He was dealing with for He had an intimate relationship with the Father—not just knowing about the Father, but knowing him on a personal level.

Somebody ought to witness that it's good to know the Lord. Somebody ought to witness that He walks with you and talks with you and lets you know that you are His child.

Grandma didn't have much education. She didn't understand all the doctrines of the Bible, but she knew that she had been converted. For, I hear her singing: "I know the Lord has laid his hands on me." It's good to know the Lord for yourself.

B. Reliance: ". . . into thy hands . . ."

Jesus, not only knew these hands, but He knew that He could trust these hands. He knew what these hands were able to accomplish. He knew the history behind these hands for He had seen these hands in action. He was there when these hands:

- scooped out the valleys and heaved up the mountains,
- hung the sun, moon, and stars in their silvery sockets like a celestial chandelier,
- scooped out a lump of clay, molded it into the shape of a human and breathed into it the breath of life.

He knew that his Father's hands were as good as his Father's word.

I must ask the question: Whose hands can you trust in difficult situations? Whose hands can you trust when things go wrong as they sometimes will? I've discovered that there are some hands you cannot trust:

- The same hands that will love you can be the same hands that will leave you.

- The same hands that will hold you can be the same hands that will hurt you.
- The same hands that will pat you on the back can be the same hands that will stab you in the back.

But, I've learned to trust the Father's hands. For the Scripture says:

- He is able to uphold you with the right hand of His righteousness,
- The right hand of the Lord doeth valiantly,
- The hand of the Lord is mighty,
- His hand will never let you fall.

His hands are:

- comforting hands, consoling hands, encouraging hands, healing hands,
- wiping tears from your eyes,
- protecting you from hurt, harm and danger,

I can trust the Father's hands. That's why I love that song:

> "I trust in God wherever I may be,
> Upon the land or on the rolling sea;
> For, come what may from day to day,
> My heavenly Father watches over me."

I can trust the Father's hands!

C. Responsibility: ". . . I commend my spirit."

Jesus knew the keeping ability of these hands. For when Jesus utters these words, it was in the hour of crisis. There He is hanging from the cross. Life's flame is growing weaker and weaker. The body is dying but the spirit is still living. And with the last ounce of energy He musters up a voice of victory, "Father, into thy hands I commend my spirit."

There are many hands that are with you when things are going well in your life, but when things turn against you, those hands are nowhere to be found. Just when you need them the most, they will toss you aside and kick you to the curb. But Jesus calls for His Father's hands because He knew that, even in a dark dilemma, these hands were competent for a crisis. For God's hands can:

- do what nobody else's can,
- reach where nobody else's can,
- hold like nobody else's can.

He can handle the urgency of an emergency. His hands:

- held open the Red Sea for Moses,
- stilled the sun for Joshua,
- brought down Goliath for David,
- stopped the lions of Daniel.

God is competent for a crisis. I can place my all in His hands for He has taken responsibility for me.

ILLUSTRATION: My son is my child. And, if I love him, because he is my child, I know that I am responsible for him. I am responsible for feeding him, clothing him, protecting him, giving him shelter, correcting him. That's my responsibility. Why? Because he is my child and I am responsible for him.

APPLICATION: And since I am God's child, through that covenant relation with Him, since He is my Father, He has taken responsibility for me. He has promised:

- to supply my every need,
- to fight my battles,
- to uphold me.

For the Bible says,

- "When you pass through the waters I will be with thee" (Isaiah 43:2);
- "Fear thou not, for I am with thee; be not dismayed, for I am your God" (Isaiah 41:10);
- "No weapon formed against thee shall prosper" (Isaiah 54:17);
- "The Lord is my Shepherd, I shall not want" (Psalm 23:1).

CONCLUSION

And because Jesus had a relationship with the Father, because He was able to rely on the Father, and because the Father had taken responsibility for Him, Jesus can cry out, "Father, I don't have much to give. I give my:

- blood to the sinners,
- back to the wood,
- head to the crown of thorns,
- clothes to the soldiers,
- hands to the nails,
- side to the spear,
- paradise to the thief,
- mother to John,

"Father, into thy hands, I commend my spirit!"

I've learned to put it all in His hands. If there is a problem that I cannot solve, I put it all in His hands. If there is a burden I cannot bear, I put it all in His hands. If there is a trial that I cannot endure, I put it all in His hands.

"If the world from you withhold of its silver and its gold,
And you have to get along with meager fare;
Just remember in his word how he feeds the little bird,
Take your burdens to the Lord and leave them there.

Leave them there, leave them there;
Take your burdens to the Lord and leave them there;
If you trust and never doubt, he'll surely bring you out,
Take your burdens to the Lord and leave them there."

OPERATION RESTORE HOPE

**"Then Peter said, 'Silver or gold I do not have, but what I have I give you.
In the name of Jesus Christ of Nazareth, rise up and walk'" (Acts 3:1-11).**

For the past several months, military personnel from the United States have been stationed in Somalia. They have been stationed there for the purpose of ensuring the safe arrival and distribution of food and medical supplies to dying people in a land that has been ravaged by poverty, civil war, and heartlessness. The mission has been aptly named "Operation Restore Hope" for the United States forces and other involved nations are called upon to bring hope in the midst of utter heartlessness and helplessness.

As the armed forces have brought hope to the people of Somalia, I submit to you today that the Church, likewise, is called upon to restore hope. The Church is called upon to perpetuate our Lord's ministry of healing and reconciliation. We are called upon to:

- be a light in darkness,
- be salt in a tasteless society,
- be an oasis in the midst of a dry desert,
- be holy in the midst of hellishness,
- be sober in the midst of drunkenness, and
- to spread a message of hope in the midst of hopelessness.

As we look at our African American communities today, we see that a sense of hopelessness exists among our people because:

- the infant mortality rate among African Americans is higher than some Third World countries,
- about 75% of black children are raised in poverty,
- 25-30% of all young black males are in prison or controlled by the prison system,
- one out of every three black marriages end in divorce, which adds to the number of families headed by single parents, with primarily the mother serving as the head of household,
- Black youth lack a sense of belonging, uniqueness and power;
- our black boys are gang-banging,
- our black girls are becoming mothers before they become women,
- our people are using, misusing, and abusing drugs,
- the halls of learning have become battlegrounds for survival, and
- drive-by shootings are just about an everyday occurrence.

Our communities are in a sad, helpless, and hopeless condition. And we must not call upon the government to do what the Church ought to be doing. We must be about our Father's business. We must bring about redemptive change in our communities. We must turn the hearts of the fathers, the mothers, and the children back to God. The more I look at it, the more convinced I am that the words of our Lord Jesus ought to be our motto:

"The Spirit of the Lord is upon me, because he has anointed me to preach the gospel to the poor, He has sent me to heal the broken hearted, to proclaim liberty to the captives and recovery of sight to the blind, to set at liberty those who are oppressed, to preach the acceptable year of the Lord" (Luke 4:18-19).

I submit to you today that this is Operation Restore Hope in action.

The words of our text gives to us an example of Operation Restore Hope. It records the first apostolic miracle. You will recall that just a few days earlier, the disciples were gathered together in the upper room in one accord in prayer. While there in that upper room, there came a sound from heaven as of a rushing mighty wind that filled the house. Cloven tongues of fire sat upon each one of them and they were all filled with the Holy Spirit and began to proclaim the wonderful works of God. Pentecost had brought about the presence and the power of the Holy Spirit.

But no sooner had the Holy Spirit been given when they were confronted with human need. Peter and James were on their way to the Temple. It was the hour of prayer, 3:00 in the afternoon, and they were rushing because they did not want to miss devotional service. Just as they were about to enter the Temple, they came across a certain lame man who was brought daily to the doorstep of the Temple to ask for alms. For forty years:

- he was in this lame condition,
- he was unable to walk,
- he needed public transportation to get where he needed to go,
- he lived in poverty having to beg for a living,
- he was in a hopeless, helpless, hapless, and hideous condition.

Every day kindhearted people would lay him not at the local bank, not at the corner tavern, not downtown, but at the gate of the Temple. It was here that he hoped to get enough money:

- to pay his rent,
- to keep his utilities on,
- to get some food for the day.

He looked for it there on the doorstep of the Temple. He knew the custom of the day. He knew it was a part of the Jewish custom to give alms. Failure of a Jew to give alms was a violation of the Law so he knew where to go. There he sat at the doorstep of the Temple expecting to receive alms from Peter and John.

Peter said to this man, "Look at us. We know what you are looking for: you are looking for some financial assistance and we are not in the position to give you what you want. But we can give you what you need. In the name of Jesus Christ of Nazareth, rise up and walk."

Peter took him by the right hand, lifted him up, and immediately his feet and ankle bones received strength. And the Bible says that he leaped up, he stood up, he walked, and he went into the Temple walking and leaping and praising God. These two uneducated followers of Christ restored hope to a life that was filled with hopelessness and despair.

The experience of Peter and John teaches us valuable lessons as we seek to be a community of hope in the midst of a broken and hopeless society.

A. We must see the condition of our communities.

Notice that Peter and John fixed their eyes on him. Here is a man who was down on his luck. Here is a man who did not have the advantages of many and was barely able to make ends meet.

Here is a man who was so far down until down began to look down on him.

But Peter and John fixed their eyes on him. They did not see him as an eyesore. They did not see him as a menace to society. They did not turn away from him, but they stopped and saw him as an individual in need of assistance. The church must be willing to see the condition of our communities.

You see, the authentic test of a Pentecostal experience, the true test of whether or not you have been born again is your response to human need. How I feel about God on Sunday is determined by how I respond to the hurts of my fellow man Monday through Saturday. One of the tragedies of the church today is that we linger so long in Acts 2 without moving to Acts 3.

- We want the delight of Pentecost but not the demands of it.
- We want the reward of Pentecost but not the responsibility.
- We want the mountaintop experience but we don't want to go into the valley.

Now, don't get me wrong. There is nothing wrong with the mountaintop experience. We need mountaintop experiences, we need that communion with God. But the longer I live, the more convinced I have become of the fact that we can become so involved in *having* church that we forget to *be* the church.

I believe this was Peter's dilemma on the Mount of Transfiguration. The mountaintop experience got so good to him that he really didn't want to let it go. But the next thing he knew, Jesus had pronounced the benediction and they were on their way back down to the valley.

My point is that the mountaintop experience and the valley experience complement each other. You cannot truly appreciate the beauty of the mountaintop unless you have been down in the valley. In the valley there is:

- discouragement, disillusionment, dejection, depression,
- hopelessness abounds,
- helplessness persists,
- broken lives exist,
- people are dying,
- children are crying,

and while we are singing about the blessed hope of the sweet by and by, we cannot neglect the present hurts of the here and now. We must see the condition of our communities.

B. We must offer a life-changing alternative.

This man was not looking for much and he really was not expecting much. All he wanted was enough to get by; something that would help him make it through the day. But deep down inside, he wanted an alternative. I can almost hear him saying, "There has got to be a better way."

The African-American community is full of folk who are looking for an alternative. They are satisfied with making it through the day but deep down inside, they really want an alternative lifestyle. They are looking for an alternative to:

- drug addiction,
- alcohol addiction,
- gang-banging,
- dead-end living,

- lonely days and sleepless nights.

If souls are to be saved, if broken lives are to be restored, if the bound are to be delivered, we must offer them the life-changing message of Jesus Christ. We must let them know that Jesus can and will change their lives.

Won't He do it? Won't He change your life? Let me call up a couple of witnesses to see if the Lord can change a life.

Come here, Zacchaeus. Will the Lord change your life? I hear him saying, "Yes, the Lord will change your life. I was minding my own business working for the IRS. I got tired of what I was doing and wanted an alternative. Then I heard that Jesus was coming my way and I wanted to get a good look at him, so I climbed up a sycamore tree. When He passed by He looked up, called me by my name and invited himself to dinner. I haven't been the same since."

Jesus will change your life.

Come here, Bartimeaus. Will the Lord change your life? I hear him saying, "Yes, the Lord will change your life. J was blind and begging along the roadside. I heard a great throng of people coming my way. I asked what was going on. Someone said that Jesus was passing by. I cried out with all the energy I had, 'Jesus, thou Son of David, have mercy on me.' You know what I found out? If you call Him loud enough, Jesus will stop by. He asked what I desired and I told him that I wanted to see. He said to me, 'Go your way, your faith has made you whole.'"

Jesus will change your life.

We must offer this life-changing alternative. We must tell a hopeless people, "In the name of Jesus Christ of Nazareth, rise up and walk."

Rise up and walk, black man! You've been castrated, exasperated, almost annihilated. You have been whipped on and lynched, and now you are killing each other. It's time for you to find another way of living. You can't blame the black woman for all your problems. You need to take charge of your own life. Rise up and walk, black man.

Rise up and walk, black woman! You have been battered and bruised often by your own men. You have been looking for love in all the wrong places. You have been relying on the love of that man to sustain you when you know that love should have brought his tail home last night. It's time for you to realize that your love and security is not found in just any man; it can only be found in the man, Christ Jesus. Rise up and walk, black woman.

Rise up and walk, black youth! You've been told what you can do and what you cannot do. You have been told by some that you are nothing and that you will never amount to anything, but I need to let you know that you are somebody. And you don't need anyone to stand up and lead you in a cheer to tell you that you are somebody. The Bible declares that if you receive Him, you have the right to be called a child of God. You are somebody because God don't make no junk. Rise up and walk, black youth.

Rise up and walk, black people! You have been oppressed, suppressed, repressed, and depressed. You have been held down for too long. Now is the time for you to stand up and be counted. In the name of Jesus Christ of Nazareth, rise up and walk!

C. We must offer a helping hand.

We cannot expect the down-trodden to get up by themselves. We must give them a helping hand. We need to help them stand on their own two feet.

Have you ever watched an ant? An ant will find a piece of food, taste it, and take a piece back to the ant colony. Before long, you will find a line of ants from the anthill to the food and from the food to the anthill. They are all pitching in to help carry that piece of food.

We must learn how to help each other. There are too many of us within our community who are trying to be stars. We go off to school, get a little bit of 'edumacation'. We take advantage of the opportunities that were afforded us. Then when we come back home, we move into the suburbs into our split level homes and split our families with our split personalities. We forget where we have come from. We forget about those who need our help.

Listen to what we say:

- I pulled myself up by my own bootstraps.
- I got mine, now you get yours.

We forget about the struggles we had to endure. But, we must offer a helping hand.

- This man was looking for a hand-out, but he got a hand offered.
- He was begging, but he got a blessing.
- He was looking for public assistance but got a piece of the action.

The lame man took Peter's hand and leaped off his bed. He took one step, he took another step, he took one more step,

- his lameness turned into leaping,
- his dreariness turned into a dance,
- his misery became a memory.

He was walking, running, jumping, leaping, and praising God. The church folk went running to see what was going on. They saw this lame man jumping and praising God. They wondered what was happening. I hear him say, "Don't mind me, I'm just trying out my new legs."

When Jesus comes into your life, something happens on the inside that makes a difference on the outside: "What a wonderful change in my life has been wrought, since Jesus came into my heart."

But, that's not the whole story. The church leaders got upset. The religious leaders got upset. They had prayed for the man, laid hands on him, and even anointed him with oil, but nothing happened. But here come two uneducated preachers speaking only twenty-six words to the man and he gets up and starts to walk. They called a council on Peter and John. They asked, "By what power do you do this?" Peter got up, full of the Holy Ghost and said, "In the name of Jesus of Nazareth this man is able to walk." There is power in the name of Jesus!

CRUMBLING FOUNDATIONS[12]

"If the foundations be destroyed, what can the righteous do?" (Psalm 11:3).

9/11 will be forever etched in our memories. For the past week, we have faced the awful reminder of the attack on the World Trade Center and the Pentagon. We can remember where we were and what we were doing when this awful news broke. Never has this sense of panic and grief hit America since that day of infamy, December 7, 1941.

Our minds have been bombarded with the images of that day. They have been rehearsed before us time and time again—how those planes were deliberately hijacked and flown into the World Trade Center, the Pentagon, and only God knows where the other one was actually intended. We've seen the panic of people as they were running in terror for their safety. We've seen the images of people who would rather jump to their death than to be caught in the fiery blaze of the attack on the World Trade Center. We've seen the images of others who were traveling from hospital to hospital looking for and hoping to find out about their loved ones, and we've heard the stories of those who spoke to their spouses for the last time.

You know the emotions that you felt: the pain, the hurt, the anger, the bitterness, as well as fear and trepidation. Now there are people who are afraid to get on the planes if they see anyone who resembles an Arab. You've heard those stories and you've seen the images.

The image that struck me the most was the image of the collapse of the World Trade Center—the upper stories of this massive building falling on victims below. To some, it symbolized a small victory over America, to see America in a defenseless state brought rejoicing in the streets of some Islamic countries. To others, it symbolized the beginning of this war on terrorism that we are presently engaged in. That which stood so massively in the New York skyline is no longer standing and lives were wiped out in a matter or moments.

Now more than ever before, the God of Abraham, Isaac, and Jacob, is being called upon. Now, more than ever before, the God of our foreparents is being called upon. And in the midst of all of this calling upon the name of the Lord, the ACLU and their supporters have been strangely silent. Now that America in the midst of a global crisis, those who proclaim as their motto, "the separation of church and state" have been silenced. And a new spirit of patriotism has now swept across America. Everybody wants to sing, "God bless America, land that I love . . ."

Why? Because now, there is the sense that we are in trouble. There is the feeling of helplessness. And now, we need a power that supersedes all other powers.

In reflecting on this, it seemed to me that the crumbling of the World Trade Center symbolized the crumbling of the American culture. For so long, America has not sensed the need for God. The reality is that it seems as if the things we have trusted in have been pulled from underneath us. The very things that America has placed its hopes in, the very things that seemed to have been the very fabric of American society, seem to have come crumbling to the ground. You must admit the fact that the God, whom this nation is calling upon now, was not on the lips of many moments before

---

[12]This sermon was preached on Sunday, September 16, 2001 in response to the terrorist attack of September 11, 2001 on the World Trade Center in New York City and the Pentagon in Washington, D.C.

those planes were hijacked.

When I looked at this vivid image, reflected and meditated on their significance, the words of the psalmist came to mind: "When the foundations are being destroyed, what can the righteous do?"

When the very core of our existence has been threatened, what can the righteous do? When that which has sustained us over the years has now been threatened, what can the righteous do? When that which we have trusted in for so long is crumbling right before our very eyes, what can the righteous do?

You have to admit the fact that we live in a society with very shaky foundations:

- When one of two marriages end in divorce.
- When couples opt out of marriage for live-in relationships with no commitment.
- When drugs and violence have overtaken our streets and neighborhoods.
- When the rich keep getting richer and the poor keep getting poorer.

The foundations are crumbling because we have trusted in things that cannot supply lasting security. In the words of the prophet Jeremiah, we have forsaken the fountain of living waters and have hewn out cisterns, broken cisterns, that can hold no water. The very things that we have trusted in have been snuffed out from under us. The rug has been pulled from underneath us and that which we felt has held us over the past decades has now, within a few minutes, been seen as less important. Resting in certain things tends to make us relax. Trusting in certain things tends to make us too comfortable. Trusting in that which ultimately cannot save tends to make us at ease in Zion.

What have we trusted in? The very things that were attacked are the very things that we have trusted in. We have trusted in our militarism—where we bully ourselves around the world. Capitalism and gross materialism where people are judged by their possessions. But more than militarism and more than capitalism, we have trusted in our personal affluence.

God takes a calculated risk every time He blesses us. The more God blesses us, the more He risks losing us. I have seen it and I know that you have seen it. When periods of difficulty come, when the trials and tribulations of this life come, there are many who will flock to God and to the church. There are many who will bust down the door of the church to get an answer to their heart's desire.

But as soon as God blesses us, we stick around long enough to say a small thank you, then we have gone on our merry way. Once we get a little somethin', we tend to think that we have pulled ourselves up by our own bootstraps.

- We forget who kept us in the midst of our difficult situations.
- We forget who kept us from dangers seen and unseen.
- We forget who provided for us when we didn't have two pennies to rub together.
- We forget who opened doors for us when they were slammed in our face.

The more God blesses us, the more He stands the risk of losing us!

The question before us is: What have you trusted in? Are you and I not Americans? Have not you and I trusted in our idols? Idols that have eyes but cannot see, ears but cannot hear, hands but cannot feel, feet but cannot walk, a mouth but cannot talk. What have you trusted in?

In examining this psalm, I discovered that this psalm is not a prayer, but is a confession of faith. It is David's response to faithless individuals who had surrounded him. The psalm says: "When the foundations are being destroyed, what can the righteous do?"

Notice what the psalm does not say. The psalm does not say, "When the foundations are being destroyed, what shall the unrighteous do."

The unrighteous are:

- the faithless,
- the doubting,
- the fickle-minded,
- the visionless,
- the weak,
- the impotent.

The unrighteous respond differently than the righteous. How do the unrighteous respond? Whenever difficulties and disappointment arise, whenever frustration and failings arise, the Scripture shows us that the unrighteous respond in two ways:

A. Flight

They say that the best way to deal with the situation is to get away from here. That was the advice given by those who surrounded David. They said that the best way to handle this situation is to take flight. Get away from here. Retreat. Get off to yourself. Get out of town before sundown, Brown. Don't place yourself at risk, for your enemy is after you. They are ready to attack you when you least expect it. They are ready to fire at you.

B. Fear

The wicked bend their bows; they set their arrows against the strings to shoot from the shadows at the upright in heart. The enemy is already upon you. You can't mess with them now. You have no other alternative.

This is a faithless person's assessment of the situation. It is a cry of despair. It is a cry of anguish. It is the cry of those who have trusted in other things to sustain them, but to no avail. And they are the ones who are saying, "If the foundations are being destroyed, what shall the righteous do?"

But David would have us know that the way to respond to a crisis situation is not flight, not fear, but in faith. David says, "I am not going to take flight. I am not going to retreat. I am not going to be fearful, but I am going to operate in faith. I will take refuge in the Lord!"

I feel you right now. You're wondering how to respond in light of these recent events, but you're also wondering how you can handle your own personal predicaments at the present time. You're wondering how you're going to make it, how you're going to take it. The answer is finding your refuge in the Lord. That's why David could say:

- "The Lord is my light and my salvation, whom shall I fear? The Lord is the strength of my life in whom shall I be afraid?" (Psalm 27:1).
- "They that trust in the Lord shall be like Mt. Zion which shall not be moved" (Psalm 125:1).
- "God is our refuge and strength, a very present help in trouble. Therefore, we shall not fear" (Psalm 46:1).
- "The Lord is my shepherd, I shall not want" (Psalm 23:1).
- "Yea, though I walk through the valley of the shadow of death, I will fear no evil for you are with me" (Psalm 23:4).

He responds in faith by finding his refuge in the God of his salvation.

Why should we take refuge in God? We should trust in God in the midst of this crisis,

A. Because of where God is seated — "The Lord is in his holy temple, the Lord's throne is in heaven" (Psalm 11:4a).

This lets us know that God reigns and is still in control. He has not relinquished His control upon the earth. The last time I checked, the earth was still the Lord's and the fullness thereof, the world and they that dwell therein. He is still the ruler of this great universe. He still sits high and looks low. He is still in charge. He is still the Master of everything. He is still the sovereign one. God is still in control!

I know there are some who believe there is no God. I know there are some who are still holding on to the theory that God is dead. I know there are even some who feel that God seems to be taking a distant seat in the situation.

But God is still in control. The days may be long and difficult. The nights may be filled with uncertainty. The road may get rough, the going may get tough, and the hills may be hard to climb, but I can make it and I can take it because the God who I serve is still on the throne!

I can make it knowing that God is in control. I can make it knowing that He rules and He super-rules. I can:

- deal with any dilemma,
- handle any heartache,
- hold on in spite of the difficulty,

knowing that God reigns. And as long as God is still on the throne, I am not worried about the future because I know that God's got it under control. God reigns!

B. Because of what God is doing ". . . his eyes behold, his eyelids try, the children of men. The Lord trieth the righteous: but the wicked and him that loveth violence his soul hateth" (Psalm 11:4b-5).

I can respond in faith knowing that God is watching over the situation. In other words, He knows what's going on. God is not a far off God. He is not so transcendent that He can't be imminent. He is not so big that He can't be concerned about our situation down here. He is not an indifferent spectator. God is not sifting back wondering what's going to happen next. He is not sitting back in a helpless state looking on with little or no interest. No! God is near and He is watching over His creation. Nothing is ignored. Nothing is overlooked. Nothing is unjudged or uncontrolled. God reigns and He rules. He's got his eyes on this situation.

Why? Because He is the all-seeing God. He sees their hatred. He sees their violence. He sees their plotting. He sees their scheming. He sees their conniving. That's how the enemy is. The enemy wants us to fall and is waiting for us to fall. The enemy is lying in wait ready to destroy us. That's why the enemy's number one weapon is fear.

But God sees their ways and He disapproves of their ways. Their time is limited, and the wicked shall receive just reward for their hatred. He sees their violence and He will judge them, which lets us know also that God is watching over His people. He loves His people and as His eye is on the wicked; His eye is also on His people. Not one hair falls from our heads without Him knowing about it. And in the midst of the trials and tribulations, He smiles upon them. This signifies God's favor upon His people. We are highly favored of God. That's why David said, "Fret not yourself because of evil doers, neither be envious of the workers of iniquity for they will soon be cut off" (Psalm 37:1).

That's why we need to learn to claim the promises of God, for all the promises of God are yes, and in Him, Amen to the glory of God. And God is not slack concerning His promises. What He says He will do; what He promises, He will perform.

- "When you pass through the waters, I will be with you and through the flood, it shall not overtake you" (Psalm 43:2);
- "No weapon formed against you shall prosper" (Isaiah 57:4);
- "No good thing will he withhold from those who trust in him" (Psalm 84:11).

Be not dismayed what e'er be tide, God will take care of you! If His eye is on the sparrow, I know He watches over me. God's got His eye on the situation!

C. Because of His character: "For the righteous Lord loveth righteousness; his countenance doth behold the upright" (Psalm 11:7).

He is the righteous Lord. Righteous is the very essence of His nature. Righteous is His name. He is a just God. He is a holy God. He is the faithful God. Perfect righteousness, wisdom and love are His. He is the righteous Lord. He loves righteousness and He looks for righteousness. How dear is righteousness to him? "He made him to be sin for us who knew no sin, that we might be made the righteousness of God in him" (2 Corinthians 5:21), which lets us know that the cross is the measure of God's love of righteousness.

And because of His righteousness, those who are upright shall see His face. This means that because of God's righteousness, we have access to the Lord.

1) Ontological Sense: We can come boldly to the throne of grace.
2) Eschatological Sense: Speaks of a future when the wicked shall cease from troubling and the weary shall be at rest.

CONCLUSION

I put my trust in the Lord. I need no other protection. I need no other refuge. For in the time of trouble he shall hide me in the secret place of his tabernacle. I can stand calmly and boldly in him knowing that "Weeping may endure for a night, but joy comes in the morning!"

WHEN ENOUGH IS ENOUGH[13]

"When Herod realized that he had been outwitted by the Magi, he was furious, and he gave orders to kill all the boys in Bethlehem and its vicinity who were two years old and under, in accordance with the time he had learned from the Magi. Then what was said through the prophet Jeremiah was fulfilled: 'A voice is heard in Ramah, weeping and great mourning, Rachel weeping for her children and refusing to be comforted, because they are no more'" (Matthew 2:16-18).

A number of years ago, Dr. T. Garrot Benjamin from Indianapolis, Indiana wrote a book entitled, *Boys to Men*, in which he depicted his concern for the youth of our community. He began this writing by articulating his pain in the form of poetry entitled, *I Hurt*.

I hurt for the precious, filled-with-potential black boys who may never become real men.

I hurt for the boys whose maturity gets raped by racism.
I hurt for boys who allow themselves to be gutted by greed.
I hurt for the boys who contract AIDS before they come of age.
I hurt for boys who get into crack before they get into church.
I hurt for boys who get into gangs before they get into God.
I hurt for boys who get into hip-hop before they get into holiness.
I hurt for boys who get into pistols before they get into prayer.
I hurt for boys who get into jail before they get into Jesus.

His aim was to express the need for us, as the people of God, to address the issues confronting our community. Around the same time, the Rev. John Cherry developed a ministry in Suitland, Maryland called "Save the Seed." The focus of this ministry was on African American males and young people. It was a rites-of-passage program designed to help young men develop into productive citizens through education and information that could bring about transformation in their lives.

These two examples are models of ministry that are vital for today. Every day we hear news of how the seed is being destroyed. I am convinced that there is a satanic conspiracy to destroy the seed. The male is the carrier of the seed. Thus, there is a satanic conspiracy to destroy the black male. Satan knows that if he can destroy the seed, if he can destroy the young people, then he can destroy an entire generation. If we are going to win the battle for the seed, we must recognize that our spiritual adversary is trying to destroy our men, children and, ultimately, our families and our people.

Based upon biblical evidence and the dangers facing this generation, we must not only save the seed, but we must do battle for the seed. There is a conspiracy to destroy the seed; and the tools used to destroy the seed are racism and violence.

I'm tired of hearing about young black men being victimized and stigmatized. I'm tired of hearing about the lives of young black men being wiped out by those who are "to protect and serve." I'm tired of the violence that takes place on the streets. There comes a time when we have to say,

---

[13]This sermon was preached at the Unity Baptist Church in Braddock, Pennsylvania on December 4, 2014 in response to the shootings of African-American men by police officers.

154

"Enough is enough. Enough of the violence. Enough of the racial profiling. Enough of the police brutality Enough of a system designed to denigrate and destroy the will of people."

"Enough is enough" is a cry of desperation. It says that what is happening must stop. It is a cry that says I can't take anymore of what's happening. I'm tired; I'm frustrated; I'm angry; I'm hurt; and I will no longer accept what is happening.

And contrary to the opinions heard on the conservative news outlets, this issue has always been in this nation and our communities for quite some time. "Enough is enough" is not just a cry of anger but also a call to action. Something must be done to stem the violence that is being launched toward black men. A strategy has to be initiated and a plan must be developed to stem this tide of violence that affects our community so deeply.

I had conversation with a ministerial colleague who shared with me a while ago that you will know when you have had enough. When you've had enough, it will move you to action. When you've had enough, you'll do something about the situation. When you've had enough, you will do what is necessary in order to make a change in your condition.

Many of us have hit that turning point. The protests around this nation and the outrage of the people have suggested that there needs to be a change. They have had enough of the racist antics across the land. They have had enough of the injustices in America, and they are expressing in their own way that "enough is enough."

The passage under consideration from Matthew 2 aptly depicts the condition of our communities. One need only read a few verses to discover that this is one of the most heartrending scenes in all of history. No one in their right mind would want to witness such a scene. It was a display of cruel, inhumane, and cold-blooded murder. Matthew recorded the innocent shedding of the blood of helpless, defenseless, and unarmed children. To think of, much less experience, the loss of a child through violence is a painful predicament.

The scenario takes place several months, possibly a year or two after the birth of Jesus. Joseph and Mary have moved from a cave to a cabin. After the excitement of the first advent, the census having been completed, things were pretty much back to normal in this little village of Bethlehem, located about ten miles south of Jerusalem.

During the course of the day Herod receives visitors. They are wise men from the East looking for one who is "born king of the Jews." They said, "We have seen his star in the East and have come to worship him."

Immediately, Herod is frightened, and all Jerusalem with him. After consulting with some of the chief priests and scribes, it was ascertained that the Scriptures spoke of one who would be born in Bethlehem. Herod urges these wise men to go to worship this king and invites them to return and let him know where this king is so that he, too, can go and worship him.

These wise men go and find Jesus, and worship Him bringing gifts. And while they rested that night at the local Comfort Inn, they were warned in a dream not to return to Herod, and went home another way.

But there is a disparity between the response of the wise men and the response of Herod. The wise men worshipped the Christ child; but Herod feared the Christ-child. Feeling that he was tricked and realizing that he been duped by these wise men, Herod goes into a fit of rage and issues a decree that all children in and around Bethlehem who are two years of age and under would be killed. There we see a deliberate plan to destroy the seed.

The Bible lets us know that this decree was carried out. Some writers have suggested that due to the size of Bethlehem, about 15-20 children were affected by this decree. Any number, whether one, twenty or two hundred, is way too many. Joseph being warned in a dream by an angel of Herod's plot, however, packed up their belongings, put Mary and Jesus on their donkey, and fled to Egypt in order to protect the child.

This child was protected. Yet, imagine the pain of the other mothers in Bethlehem. Imagine the agony of these mothers as they held their children who were lying dead in cold blood. Imagine these mothers trying to come to grips with those senseless killings. Imagine those mothers trying to understand why this had to happen to their child and refusing to be consoled. It was described as Rachel weeping for her children and refusing to be consoled because the anguish was too much to bear.

This is a scene all too real in our society. It seems like a waste of life. It seems like an immense waste of God's creation that one would, so here is the strategy that must be implemented in order to stem the tide in our society and deal with this culture of violence. The narrative shows us what we can do.

1. Realize who we are dealing with.

Herod was an Idumean in race, a descendant from Edom (Esau) who was a Jew in his religion, a heathen in practice and a monster in character. There was a history with Herod. If you look at his life, you will see that he got to where he was due to some political ties, friendships, and ruthlessness, prepared to commit any crime in order to gratify his unbounded ambition, Herod was granted the title of "King of Judea" by the Roman Senate. As such, he was a vassal of the Roman Empire, expected to support the interests of his Roman patrons.

He suffered from depression and paranoia. He was fearful, jealous, insecure, and eliminated any threat to his power, even from his own deathbed. Whenever one's sense of authority is threatened, they will exert force to ensure control. They go into rage, first through their words (threats), then through their violence.

Herod represents a system of hatred and bigotry that seeks to destroy a race of people. We saw it when Pharaoh sought to destroy the Israelites. We saw it in the period of slavery and segregation—a period perpetuated by a attitude of supremacy in the dominant culture. You have to recognize who you are dealing with—we wrestle not against flesh and blood . . .

The faces associated with these senseless killings are just symptoms of the real American problem. The real problem is a system of racism that permeates American culture. The system blames African Americans for the social ills in America. It's a system that says that claims our current president is the cause for the racism in society, but failing to realize that the issue has always been there; it just raised its ugly head since he's been in office.

It is the system that claims black-on-black crime is the major social ill of our society, when mass shootings, extortion and white collar crimes are just as prevalent within the dominant culture as there is "black-on-black" crime. It's a system that is designed to look at blacks with suspicion. It's a system that labels all black males as gang-bangin', baby-makin', gangsta rappin', system breakin' thugs.

We are fighting a system that is not just in its dealings, a system designed to enslave and to disenfranchise people of color, regardless of their ethnicity.

It's genocide. It's a prevalent part of today's society. There is a deliberate act on the part of the Herods of this world to destroy people of color. It is an intentional act by one who is seeking to thwart the purpose of God in a life. It is a slaughter, not just of a physical nature, but an emotional, mental, and psychological slaughter of the souls of black men. It's a mind control. And the enemy knows that the best way to destroy a race is to destroy the seed by messing with the mind. For if you mess with the mind, you can destroy the will.

That's why our young boys don't expect to live past the age of 25. It's a conspiracy to destroy our boys, fostered by a racist system that teaches us to hate ourselves. A system that teaches us that certain among us are worthless and will never amount to anything. The real problem is not a skin issue, it's a sin issue.

2. Raise our own level of consciousness.

We cannot blame the system for all of our problems. For, if the truth be told, are we not guilty of contributing to this conspiracy? If we recognize that we are fighting a system designed to destroy, then there is the onus/burden of personal responsibility and accountability. If we recognize that we are fighting a system of racism, then don't give the system what they want.

We tend to blameshift and place the blame on other things when it's not the things that do it, it's us. Are we not guilty of contributing to the conspiracy when we speak a language of hatred to our children and at their fathers? Are we not guilty of fostering this conspiracy when we engage in a lifestyle that is antithetical to the destiny that God intended for us?

In other words, it's a family affair—the whole family is involved in the process. The children sell the crack, the father makes the deal, and the mothers cook the crack. We place the blame of the illicit drugs that are in the communities. We place the blame on the illegal guns in the community.

However, the supply only meets the demands. Are we not aiding and abetting the conspiracy to destroy us? Are we not killing our own selves and our own children? Are we not robbing ourselves of the destiny that God has for us? Quit playing the victim if you are the one who is victimizing! We have to take responsibility for our actions.

3. We must foster a culture of hope.

Rachel, the mothers of today, refuse to be comforted. They cannot deal with the prospects of losing a child to violence. They cannot handle the concept of losing their child to drugs. She refuses to be consoled.

This is a sign of hopelessness. This is a sign of resignation: giving up and not doing anything about the situation. Why? Because they are so overtaken by grief that they cannot see a remedy for the situation. All too often the African American community accepts its problems as insurmountable, not understanding that systemic racism and oppression are designed to foster this type of passive resignation. Too often we see the situation as hopeless, but God has already given us the power to do something about it.

Enough is enough. No more of this. Too many have chosen to write off the youth of our community. We have given up on them and said by our words and our actions that there is no hope for them. We have given up on them for we see them as having no hope, no future, and no life. It's seen in our antagonistic attitudes toward our own youth It's seen in our unwillingness to listen to the hurts they are experiencing

But it is bad theology to give up on anybody. To give up on anyone suggests that God does not have the power to save from the guttermost to the uttermost. To give up on anyone suggests that God is powerless to do anything about the human situation.

We should never give up on anyone, for the reality is that there were some folk who never really gave up on you. There were some folk who wanted to give up on you. There were some folk who were ready to write you off. They said you were nothing and would never amount to anything. But some sainted grandmother, some devout mother, some godly father did not give up on you. They saw something in you that you didn't see in yourself. They took the time to pray for you. They invested themselves in you. They disciplined and trained you, and look where you are today. You're still holding on to God's hand.

This lets us know that in a community where hopelessness seems to abound, we must counteract that sense of hopelessness. It's a call for us to rise up and be counted—to present change in our communities and in society that says, "We ain't taking no more of this! Enough is enough!"

Yes, we have been victimized by a racist society that sees black lives as nothing; but be careful not to internalize the victimization. You may crush me down; but I'm still breathing! "We are hard pressed on every side, but not crushed; perplexed, but not in despair; persecuted, but not abandoned; struck down, but not destroyed" (2 Corinthians 4:8).

I'm still breathing!

The church is called upon to be the conscience of the community, and to make a conscious effort to protect the seed. Is there risk involved? Yes, there is risk. There is the risk of being rejected. There is the risk of being ridiculed, but it's a risk worth taking. Why? Because each child is a child of destiny. Eugene Perkins calls African American children "the seeds of our destiny and ultimate liberation." There is hope for each child and each life is worth the effort to save.

We may not save all of them, but if we can save one at a time, it's worth the effort. That's what happened in the divine scheme of things. Herod's plan was to destroy this would-be king of the Jews, but God divinely delivered this Christ-child. If God had not sent an angel to warn Joseph of Herod's plan, the plan of salvation could have been destroyed. The Anointed One would have been annihilated.

But this Christ child was saved, and this child turned out to be the Savior of the world. It was this child who came to destroy the works of the devil. It was this child who came to seek and to save that which was lost. It was this child who turned out to be the transformer of generations of people.

Save the seed for "enough is enough!"

EPILOGUE

As I stated at the beginning of this collection, Black preaching is among the strongest preaching on the American scene. The preaching of the Black cleric has been known to inspire, challenge, motivate, and transform the lives of the hearers. Though there are those who make a mockery of it, when push comes to shove, they enjoy and sometimes crave Black preaching.

As I read through this collection of sermons once one more time, I was once again impressed with our hermeneutic flexibility and homiletic ingenuity. While we preached decades apart from one another, my grandfather, father, uncle and I all addressed the needs of the day, taking the passage and applying it in such a way that everyone could go home with some helpful tips on how to apply the Word to their situation. As I read through these messages, I made another commitment to continue to be relevant as well as grounded in the biblical truth that my family has cherished for three generations.

As previously noted, I had never heard my grandfather preach. My recollections of both my father and uncle grow fainter with each passing year. Each one's preaching style was unique to his own personality. Each of us mostly utilized the three-point outline, though I recall my father being less definitive in the delineation of his points. Or, it could have been that he was subtler with his moves than the others.

I hope you noticed that each individual climax in each sermon was distinct. I wish I had been able to capture the enthusiasm with which the messages were received along with the response of the listeners, for what makes Black preaching so special is the involvement of the people. Uniquely attributed to the African American religious tradition is the call/response, a pattern of spontaneous interaction in which expressions, both verbal and nonverbal, are used to encourage and affirm the truth being proclaimed. In recollection, I hear my father saying, "Don't you see it?" or my uncle saying, "Say amen somebody." The responses are not simply tradition, but the witness of the Spirit ringing through their "Hallelujahs" or "Thank You, Jesus," or "Glory to God" or "Preach it, brother" to indicate that truth was being spoken. L. H. Welchel, Jr. refers to it as, "a dynamic discourse between the pulpit and the congregation which is more reflective of African spirituality than European spirituality."

Of course, what is not included is the adlib that went beyond the manuscript, or the tonal variety, body language, and facial expressions that went with each sermon's delivery. I wish I had my family on video, but I do have some reel-to-reel messages from the past that hopefully one day I will get around to converting and then transcribing. Maybe that will be my next book

All who preach the gospel seek to balance the demands of Scripture and the social needs of the day. We realize that what we are using as our source was written thousands of years ago, but is still living and breathing, and able to speak to the needs of every generation, including ours. While we are Black preachers with a Black preaching heritage and style, we are preaching a timeless gospel that is relevant — and desperately needed — by every ethnic group and culture of our day. The gospel is not just for the down-and-outer, but the up-and-outer as well. While our audience may tend to be of one unique group, we must design our messages so they can be universally applied.

To God be the glory for the work we have done, and I pray, like Nehemiah, "Remember me for this, my God, and do not blot out what I have so faithfully done for the house of my God and its services" (Nehemiah 13:14).

www.ingramcontent.com/pod-product-compliance
Lightning Source LLC
Chambersburg PA
CBHW062043090426

42740CB00016B/3006